JAZZY
GIFT BASKETS

JAZZY
GIFT BASKETS

MAKING & DECORATING GLORIOUS PRESENTS

Marie Browning

Sterling Publishing Co., Inc.
New York

Prolific Impressions Production Staff:
Editor in Chief: Mickey Baskett
Copy Editor: Phyllis Mueller
Graphics: Dianne Miller, Karen Turpin
Styling: Marie Browning
Photography: Visions West Photography, John Yanyshyn
Administration: Jim Baskett

Library of Congress Cataloging-in-Publication Data
Browning, Marie.
    Jazzy gift baskets : making & decorating glorious presents / Marie Browning.
        p. cm.
    Includes index.
    ISBN 1-4027-1472-6
    1. Gift baskets. I. Title.
TT157.B7854 2005
745.59--dc22

2005018892

10 9 8 7 6 5 4 3 2 1

Published in paperback in 2007 by Sterling Publishing Co., Inc.
387 Park Avenue South, New York, N.Y. 10016
© 2006 by Prolific Impressions, Inc.
Produced by Prolific Impressions, Inc.
160 South Candler St., Decatur, GA 30030
Distributed in Canada by Sterling Publishing
c/o Canadian Manda Group, 165 Dufferin Street,
Toronto, Ontario, Canada M6K 3H6
Distributed in the United Kingdom by GMC Distribution Services,
Castle Place, 166 High Street, Lewes, East Sussex, England BN7 1XU
Distributed in Australia by Capricorn Link (Australia) Pty. Ltd.
P.O. Box 704, Windsor, NSW 2756 Australia

Printed in China
All rights reserved

Sterling ISBN-13: 978-1-4027-1472-6 Hardcover
        ISBN-10: 1-4027-1472-6

        ISBN-13: 978-1-4027-4442-6 Paperback
        ISBN-10: 1-4027-4442-0

For information about custom editions, special sales, premium and corporate purchases, please contact Sterling Special Sales Department at 800-805-5489 or specialsales@sterlingpub.com.

Acknowledgments

I would like to thank the following manufacturers for their generous contributions of quality products and support in the creation of the projects in this book:

For craft glues:
Beacon Adhesives, Mt. Vernon, NY, USA; www.beaconadhesives.com

For metal charms:
Boutique Trims, South Lyon, MI, USA; www.boutiquetrims.com

For beads, findings, charms, and pendants: Blue Moon Beads, Van Nuys, CA, USA; www.bluemoonbeads.com

For acrylic paints, acrylic mediums, and acrylic varnishes:
Delta Technical Coatings, Whittier, CA, USA, www.deltacrafts.com

For melt and pour soap bases, colorants, fragrances, and soap molds: Environmental Technologies, Fields Landing, CA, USA; www.eti-usa.com

For scissors, rotary cutters, and general tools:
Fiskars Brands, Inc., Wausau, WI, USA; ww.fiskars.com

For colored wire:
JewelCraft LLC, Secaucus, NJ, USA; www.jewelcraft.biz

For spray paints and varnishes:
Krylon, Cleveland, OH, USA; www.krylon.com

For decoupage medium, acrylic paints, acrylic mediums, and acrylic varnishes: Plaid Enterprises, Inc., Norcross, GA, USA; www.plaidonline.com

For paint brushes and sponges:
Royal Brush, Merrillville, IN, USA; www.royalbrush.com

For spray-on, non-expanding floral foam: Softroc, Pittsburgh, PA, USA; www.softroc.com

MEET THE AUTHOR
Marie Browning

Marie Browning is a consummate craft designer who has made a career of designing products, writing books and articles, and teaching and demonstrating. You may have been charmed by her creative acumen but not been aware of the woman behind it - Marie has designed stencils, stamps, transfers, and a variety of other award-winning product lines for art and craft supply companies. In addition to writing numerous books on creative living, Marie's articles and designs have appeared in myriad home decor and crafts magazines.

Marie Browning earned a Fine Arts Diploma from Camosun College and attended the University of Victoria.

She is a Certified Professional Demonstrator, a design member of the Crafts and Hobby Association (CHA), and a member of the Society of Craft Designers (SCD). Marie serves on the SCD's trend committee, which researches and writes about upcoming trends in the arts and crafts industry. In 2004, she was selected by *Craftrends,* a trade publication, as a "top influential industry designer."

She lives, gardens, and crafts on Vancouver Island in Canada. She and her husband Scott have three children: Katelyn, Lena, and Jonathan. Marie can be contacted at www.mariebrowning.com

Books by Marie Browning Published by Sterling

Purse Pizzazz (2005)

More Jazzy Jars (2005)

Totally Cool Polymer Clay for Kids (2005)

Totally Cool Soapmaking for Kids (2004)

Wonderful Wraps (2003, re-printed in soft-cover)

Jazzy Jars (2003, re-printed in soft-cover)

Designer Soapmaking (2003, re-printed in German)

300 Recipes for Soap (2002, re-printed in soft-cover and in French)

Crafting with Vellum & Parchment (2001, re-printed in soft-cover with the title *New Paper Crafts*)

Melt & Pour Soaps (2000, re-printed in soft-cover)

Hand Decorating Paper (2000, re-printed in soft-cover)

Memory Gifts (2000, re-printed in soft-cover with the title *Family Photocrafts*)

Making Glorious Gifts from Your Garden (1999, re-printed in soft-cover)

Handcrafted Journals, Albums, Scrapbooks & More (1999, re-printed in soft-cover)

Beautiful Handmade Natural Soaps (1998, re-printed in soft-cover with the title *Natural Soapmaking*)

Give the Gift of a Decorated Basket

At birthdays, holidays, and other gift-giving occasions, gift baskets are the answer - they make it easy to create a memorable and creative gift, help to keep down costs, and are appropriate for almost any recipient. Gift baskets present personalized, home-crafted gifts in a dramatic way that brings joy, excitement, and delight. Best of all, a basket filled to overflowing with tantalizing treats and wrapped in shiny cellophane is almost as much fun to make as it is to receive. It's a gift of your time, thought, and creativity.

Gift baskets custom created by you and given from the heart will always be appreciated and remembered. This book shows you a variety of techniques for decorating baskets and presents a wealth of ideas for selecting, handcrafting, and creatively packaging gifts. More than two dozen gift basket projects are included, along with recipes and projects instructions for gifts and ideas for other basket themes.

custom created by you and given from the heart

When making your own gift baskets you celebrate your originality by personalizing the basket to suit the recipient, and you can save money by making your own food mixes, bath products, and accessories. Let these projects inform and inspire your gift baskets, and let your imagination run wild!

Decorated Baskets in Home Decor

Decorated baskets are gifts in themselves - they create a wonderful presentation and can be used as storage containers or home accents after the contents are enjoyed. When I began writing this book, I was amazed at the number of baskets I have in my home! Baskets come in many different shapes, sizes, and colors. They can fit in any decor theme, from Asian modern to cozy country, adding texture, cultural interest, and color to rooms.

By adding a decorative rim of silk flowers, a new painted finish, or a decoupaged motif, you can convert any basket into a beautiful home decor accent that is both artistic and useful. A decorated basket that matches your decor is a great way to increase storage space while keeping things attractive. Baskets work in bathrooms, bedrooms, kitchens, and casual and formal living areas. Fabric linings can dress up a basket for display on shelves or in an open cupboard. Decorated baskets can hold magazines, bath items, or clothing or be filled with potpourri or fragrant pine cones. The decorative possibilities are endless.

A Gift Basket Business

Gift baskets are a multi-million-dollar industry, listed in small business periodicals among the top ten home-based businesses. A gift basket business is flexible - it can be started small and built to be any size the owner wants, from a part-time service with minimal resources to a storefront with seven-day-a-week, full service availability.

The gift basket trade is not a new business, but it continues to grow and is a wonderful way for people to build personal and business relationships, encouraging and supporting employees and loved ones.

The gift basket trade... continues to grow...

Fundraising with Gift Baskets

Gift baskets are a great way to package items for raffles, offering a showy and impressive display sure to sell lots of tickets for your event. For sports tournaments, try loading theme baskets with donated items from local merchants, wrapped with cellophane and displayed with a covered container. Sell raffle tickets, allowing participants to place their tickets in the containers for the baskets they hope to win. Design different themes for children, men, and women so everyone can choose a favorite. Theme baskets showcasing participating businesses can be created for fun events and generate heaps of funds for your chosen charity.

BASKETS AS GIFT CONTAINERS

Baskets are generally made by weaving natural fibers to form a container and come in a wide range of colors, shapes and sizes. There is also a wide choice in the kind of handles, from metal to vine.

The main categories of baskets are:

Coiled baskets, made with soft grasses and rushes.

Plaited baskets, made with soft, flexible materials that are wide and ribbon-like, such as palm fronds or yucca leaves.

Twined baskets, made from roots or vines and twisted materials such as rope.

Wicker baskets, made with reed, cane, and willow.

Splint baskets, made with thin strips of oak, ash, and bamboo.

Basketry is an ancient craft, said to be the oldest. Our ancestors, no matter who or where they were, made baskets. In every civilization and every part of the world, basket making has been practiced. Basket making survives in many parts of the world today in forms, techniques, and materials similar to those used in ancient times.

Baskets are available in a wide range of colors, shapes and sizes. There is also a wide choice in the kind of handles, from metal to vine.

Basket dimensions given in this book state the length and width of the basket at its largest dimensions, plus the height. Unless stated otherwise, height measurements include the handle.

Other Containers

In this book, I have used traditional baskets as the project containers, decorating and embellishing them with a variety of techniques. However, other containers can be used. For a garden theme gift, consider a large plant pot or a clay saucer. For food gifts, try large bowls, colanders, or even a cookie sheet. A child's gift basket can start with a sand pail, a toy truck, or a small wagon.

TOOLS & CRAFTING SUPPLIES
for creating gift baskets

■ Cutting & Measuring Tools

- **Sharp craft scissors** are needed for cutting small pieces and decorative treatments such as ribbons and trims. They are also used for cutting out paper pieces and images for decoupage.
- **Large shears** are used for cutting fabric.
- **Rotary cutter** is used for cutting fabric to make into ribbons.
- **Metal ruler** is needed along with the rotary cutter for cutting straight edges.
- **Cutting mat** is handy to have when using the rotary cutter.
- **Measuring tape** is a good choice for exact measuring, especially when measuring along curved areas.

■ Brushes & Painting Tools

- **Flat Brushes:** You will need a variety of 1/2" and 1" flat brushes for painting the baskets. Baskets are hard on brush bristles; choose good quality brushes - their bristles are less likely to fall out.
- **Sea Sponge**: Fine textured sea sponges can be used for fast basecoating and sponged finishes.
- **Other general painting supplies include:** paper towels, low-tack masking tape, a water basin, and brush cleaner soap.

Continued on next page

Tools & Crafting Supplies, continued

■ Adhesives

Using the proper adhesives for the surfaces is important for successful projects. The adhesives you use should hold up with normal use and hold your embellishments tight even if the basket is handled roughly.

- **Hot glue gun with clear glue sticks** is used when an instant, strong bond is required for applying trims, silk flowers, or embellishments - it's easy and quick to use and is waterproof. Apply a thin stream of glue or a small dab and adhere the item immediately. A glue gun is not suitable for attaching some heavier items, as it does not hold up with repeated use. And hot glue won't allow repositioning or removal if something is glued in the wrong place. Always use the stand to keep the gun sitting upright at your work station, and keep the glue sticks in a cup to prevent them from rolling around.

- **Thick, tacky white craft glue** is used for heavier embellishments and creates a stronger bond than hot glue. White glue, however, can release items if the basket gets wet or if conditions are too humid.

- **Thin-bodied white craft glue** or **decoupage finish** is excellent for adding paper napkins to baskets and mixing with Spanish moss to construct a base for arranging silk or dried flowers. Look for sepia-toned or pearlized decoupage mediums for greater design possibilities.

- **Glue dots** are small drops of extra strength glue that come on a paper roll. They are great for holding individual items in place.

- Specialty craft glues, such as **fabric glue**, **jewelry glue**, and **wood glue**, work best for specific situations, such as using jewelry glue for attaching buttons and charms or fabric glue for attaching a fabric lining. **Stop-fray glue** - the kind that stops cut edges of fabrics and cord ends from fraying - is also valuable. It's white when wet and dries crystal clear.

■ Tools

- **Wire cutters** and **needlenose pliers** are essential when working with wire. They are also useful to cut back the basket to insert wire handles or to cut or pull off unwanted handles.

■ Paints & Mediums

- **Spray paints** come in a wide variety of colors and finishes and dry quickly. Small cans are great for small projects and for creating a variegated color spray on a basket. Follow the manufacturer's directions for use.

- **Acrylic craft paints** offer transparent or opaque coverage and come in a wide range of colors. Do not thin acrylic paints with water - instead, use a **gel medium** manufactured for that brand of paint to create a stain or glaze.

- **White-tinted acrylic varnish** adds a soft whitewashed effect on baskets.

- **Acrylic varnishes** are available in a variety of sheens. You will need these to finish and protect your decorated basket surfaces. While still wet, acrylic paints and varnishes clean up easily with soap and water. When dried and cured, they are durable and waterproof.

■ Floral Foam

- **Brick-type floral foam** is needed in the basket construction.

- **Spray-on floral foam** that is non-expanding is also used. This easy-to-work-with foam comes in colors and can be applied to the front or rim of a basket to form a base for arranging silk or dried flowers. The foam is durable when dry. Follow the manufacturer's directions for application carefully, and wear gloves to protect your hands.

Pictured above: Tools & Equipment, 1. Glue gun, 2. Glue sticks, 3. Adhesives, 4. Spray floral foam, 5. Spray paint, 6. Acrylic craft paints, 7. Acrylic painting mediums, 8. Needlenose pliers and wire cutters, 9. Paint brush, 10. Sea sponge, 11. Large shears, 12. Small sharp scissors, 13. Rotary cutter

TRIMS & EMBELLISHMENTS
for decorating baskets

■ Fabric

Fabric is used to create basket linings, both sewn and glued, as well as for making fabric ribbon. For best results, use 100% cotton and cotton-polyester blends, and avoid heavy fabrics like terrycloth and fabrics with a heavy nap, such as velvet. Fabrics also can be decoupaged on splint-type baskets.

■ Ribbons

Ribbons are by far the easiest trims to work with and match to a project, though it can be overwhelming to select a ribbon from the extensive variety available at fabric and craft stores. Satin, paper, fabric, wire-edge, and natural fiber ribbons are my favorites to work with when creating gift baskets. Collect ribbons in a wide variety of widths, styles, textures, and colors so you have lots to choose from when you're assembling your baskets.

Raffia comes both natural and colored. There is also an imitation raffia ribbon that is easy to work and produces a similar look. **Paper ribbon** comes in tight coils and uncoiled versions that are 3" to 6" wide. I prefer to unwind the coils myself. Paper ribbon can easily be cut in a variety of widths. A great technique is to paint coiled paper ribbon with acrylic paint - use a sponge to apply a thin layer of paint to the coil, hang to dry, and carefully unravel to reveal random streaks of color.

■ Trims & Tassels

Braid, rickrack, decorative fibers, and other trims are available in a great variety of widths, textures, and colors in both sewing and home decor sections.

You'll find a selection of tassels at home decor, fabric, and craft outlets. You can embellish purchased tassels with beads, other trims, or ribbon roses. You can also make your own tassels by winding and gluing 3"- to 4"-long lampshade fringe or bead fringe around the knotted end of a 10" piece of cord - simply place a line of fabric glue along the top edge of the fringe and tightly wrap around the cord end.

■ Embellishments

Simple extra embellishments make a decorated basket look professional and finished. Here are some of my favorites; find them at your local craft store or fabric store.

Beads, buttons, ribbon roses, charms, and label frames are available in a great abundance in a wide range of colors, finishes, and motifs. Use jewelry glue to adhere them. Use **colored wire** as both a tool and for decorating baskets - 20- or 22-gauge wire is easy to work with and holds shapes well. Heavier 18-gauge wire can be used for creating basket handles.

■ Silk Flowers & Artificial Fruits

All parts of silk flowers and artificial fruits can be used to decorate baskets - flower heads and individual petals can be used off the stem and arranged to cover the rim or as an all-over decoration. Leaves and fruit can be trimmed from the stem and used in the same way. Save all those stems after you strip off the flowers and greenery - they make great basket handles.

TIP: To scent silk or dried flowers, add a few drops of fragrance oil to the backs of the blossoms. Always test the oil first in a hidden area; oils can stain silk flowers.

■ Decorative Papers

For decoupage, my favorite material is paper napkins. They are available in a wide assortment of colors and themes and are thin enough to be formed around the weave of a basket. Napkins with a light or white background are translucent when decoupaged on baskets, letting natural tones show through. Decoupage papers and stickers are great for decorating flat basket tops and flat-sided wooden baskets.

Pictured above: 1. Fabric, 2. Ribbons, 3. Raffia, natural and dyed, 4. Paper ribbon, 5. Trim, 6. Tassel, 7. Charms,
8. Label frames, 9. Buttons, 10. Colored wire, 11. Beads, 12. Ribbon roses, 13. Silk flowers, 14. Artificial fruit, 15. Branches,
16. Paper napkins

BASKET WRAPPING SUPPLIES

Wrapping gives a finished look to a gift basket and helps keep the contents secure. Using a clear or sheer material allows the recipient to view the contents. When you have decorated your basket, gathered the gifts, and you're ready to assemble the gift basket, you'll need these materials:

Cellophane comes in a variety of widths, the most popular being 20", 24" and 30". I mainly use clear cellophane to wrap baskets, but it is also available in different transparent colors, in holographic or iridescent styles, and printed with designs.

Shrink-wrap is used by professional gift basket creators. It is found pre-formed in a basic basket shape in small, medium, and large sizes. You use a heat gun to shrink the wrap around the basket; the wrap gains strength as it shrinks for a sturdy, professional finish. Look for basket shrink-wraps in craft stores and floral shops.

Tulle, which is available in wide rolls, gives a romantic, elegant look. You can find different colors of tulle, both plain and with sparkles, pearls, or small jewels, at fabric and craft stores.

Clear tape is used to tape back excess cellophane or close openings - it's almost undetectable on cellophane. Frosted tape for wrapping parcels doesn't hold cellophane well and is not invisible.

Twist ties are the easiest way to quickly secure cellophane - much easier than tying a string or ribbon and easier for the recipient to open. I like to use gold or colored twist ties to tie up cellophane bags full of goodies - find them at packaging stores and candy and cake decorating stores. You can substitute **chenille stems** for twist ties; they're available at craft stores.

■ Special Packaging Supplies

• **Floral bags** are cellophane bags that come in cone shapes to hold flower or herb bouquets. Look for them at florist's shops.

• **Cellophane bags**, available clear or printed, come in different sizes and quality. Having a range of bags makes it easy to quickly re-package items or package homemade goodies. I like to use clear, crisp cellophane bags, but plastic ones are nice for food items. Look for these bags at candy and cake-making stores, kitchen shops, or craft outlets.

■ Bases & Stuffing

Bases and stuffing materials provide a sturdy platform for displaying items so they're visible above the rim of the basket. Shreds help to hide the base and add a decorative quality. Here are some examples:

Brick floral foam provides a sturdy, flat platform and a base for anchoring articles in a gift basket. Brick floral foam comes in two types - one for use with dried materials and one you soak in water and use for arranging fresh flowers. For gift baskets, always use the type designed for dried arrangements. For large baskets, join two bricks by pushing a few wooden skewers through them. You can easily saw the bricks to fit into low baskets with a large serrated knife. Wrapping floral foam bricks with tissue paper keeps bits from rubbing off, especially when you're using cut pieces.

Wooden skewers are a very handy material. Hot glue them to articles and push the skewers into floral foam to hold and arrange items decoratively. I buy 10" skewers and cut them to size with wire cutters as needed. Cut the skewer at an angle to provide a sharp point. To make them less noticeable, paint them using a sponge and acrylic paint. TIP: Place **clear tape** on small packages before gluing the skewer in place - then the skewer can be peeled off without tearing the package.

Continued on page 18

Pictured above: Basket Construction Supplies, 1. Brick floral foam, 2. Brown kraft paper, 3. Recycled paper shreds, 4. Twist ties, 5. Wooden skewers, 6. Cellophane bags, 7. Tissue shreds, 8. Metallic shreds, 9. Pleated paper shreds, 10. Natural excelsior, 11. Clear tape, 12. Clear cellophane, 13. Lazy susan

Basket Wrapping Materials, continued

Brown kraft paper - the type that comes on rolls for mailing parcels - is my favorite base material. To use, crumple large pieces into tight wads and place in the basket. The brown color blends with the basket; it also holds brick floral foam pieces securely. You can also use **recycled newspaper** as a base - it is more economical than brown paper, but not as sturdy, and the ink can smear on your hands and the items in your basket. For large baskets, use newspaper on the bottom of the basket and cover with pieces of brown paper.

Recycled paper shreds, from your own shredder or from offices that shred useless documents, work well as a base in smaller baskets and can be used in combination with brown paper for deeper baskets. The shreds are easy to form into pockets for holding heavier items such as bottles.

Decorative shreds come in a variety of colors and types, including bright metallic ones. Pleated paper shreds work especially well to hide the base, and a small amount goes a long way. I sometimes use small pieces of wire to secure shreds to the brick floral foam and to keep the shreds in place; most of the time, I just place small bunches between items. You can make your own decorative shreds in custom colors by running tissue paper through a paper shredder.

Natural excelsior is a favorite for casual or country-theme baskets. Again, a little goes a long way.

Optional: A **lazy susan** allows you to quickly assess the basket from all views and get to the back without lifting. It is also handy when decorating the basket rim with silk flowers.

PAINTING A BASKET

Spray Paint

Spray paint is a wonderful way to quickly color a basket. Two coats are usually sufficient.

To create a two- or three-toned variegated color spray, start with the lightest color and completely cover the basket with two coats of paint. Use other colors to spray bands of color around the basket for a shaded effect. To avoid unsightly paint drips, don't over-spray. You can also stain a basket with spray paint by wiping the surface with a paper towel immediately after spraying. CAUTION: Apply spray paint in a ventilated room or outdoors. Cover your surface well. Before using a spray-painted basket to hold food or scented items, let it dry and cure at least 48 hours. If you use it right away, you run the risk of tainting items with paint fumes.

Staining

Staining adds subtle color and allows the basket's natural beauty to show. Use acrylic wood stains for traditional wood hues or mix equal amounts of acrylic paint and a gel medium to create your own tint. TIP: Test the mix on the bottom of the basket.

To apply stain, use a broad brush or sponge and wipe on a thin layer, then immediately wipe off the excess with a paper towel. Let dry, then sand lightly to bring out the weave and give the basket a smooth finish. To darken the color, apply a second coat. Apply acrylic varnish before painting on a stained basket or gluing on embellishments.

Whitewashing

Whitewashing (pickling) is done like staining, but a white or light-colored wash is used. You can buy a whitewashing product that colors and varnishes in one easy step, or make your own by mixing equal amounts of white acrylic paint and acrylic matte varnish.

Distressing

For an aged look, you can distress a spray painted, stained, or whitewashed basket. Use medium (100 grit) sandpaper to lightly sand the surface and highlight the weave. After sanding, wipe the surface with a soft cloth, then apply a coat of varnish.

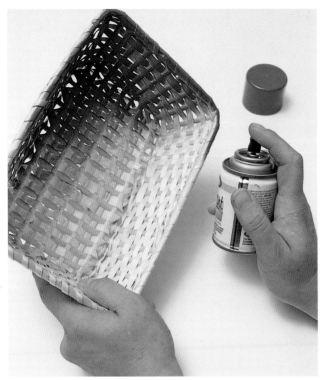

Spray painting

Whitewashing

Distressing

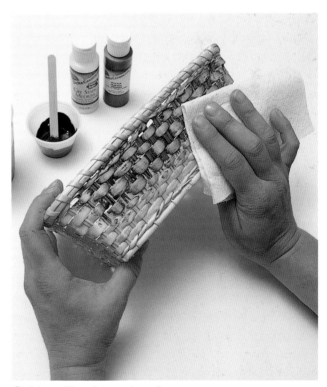

Staining with paint + gel medium

DECOUPAGE

Paper Decoupage

I like to use paper napkins to decoupage baskets. The thin, printed top layer of a paper napkin blends into the weave of the basket - it doesn't just sit on top. A paper napkin with a white background appears transparent when decoupaged, allowing the natural basket color to show through. For wooden basket tops and other smooth surfaces, motifs cut from paper or stickers can be used.

1. Cut & Tear:

For paper napkins: Remove any extra paper by simply pulling it away from the printed layer of the napkin; then carefully tear around the image you wish to use. The torn edges blend into each other, making joints practically invisible. TIP: For more precise tearing, use a brush and clean water to paint a water line on the napkin where you want to tear it, then pull the napkin carefully to tear along the wet edge.

For other paper images: Trim away excess paper around the motif, then use a craft knife and cutting mat to remove inside areas before cutting around the outer edges. Use small, sharp, pointed scissors to cut out the images, moving the paper, not the scissors, as you cut and holding the scissors at a 45-degree angle to create a tiny beveled edge. This edge helps the image fit snugly against the surface.

2. Glue:

Cover your working surface with freezer paper to protect it.

For thin papers, such as paper napkins and fine handmade papers, brush decoupage medium on the surface and attach the paper piece. Immediately brush the medium over the paper to adhere. Smooth out any wrinkles.

For sturdier papers and paper motifs, lightly coat the back of the image with decoupage medium, position on the surface, and smooth with your fingers, pushing out wrinkles and air bubbles. Allow to dry.

Fabric Decoupage

You can also cover a basket with fabric decoupage. Choose 100% cotton fabric and a basket with a simple plaited or splint construction. Cut the fabric into strips and use the basic decoupage technique - apply the medium to the back of the fabric, place it on the surface, then brush with another coat of medium. Let dry.

Using the printed top layer of a paper napkin to decoupage a basket.

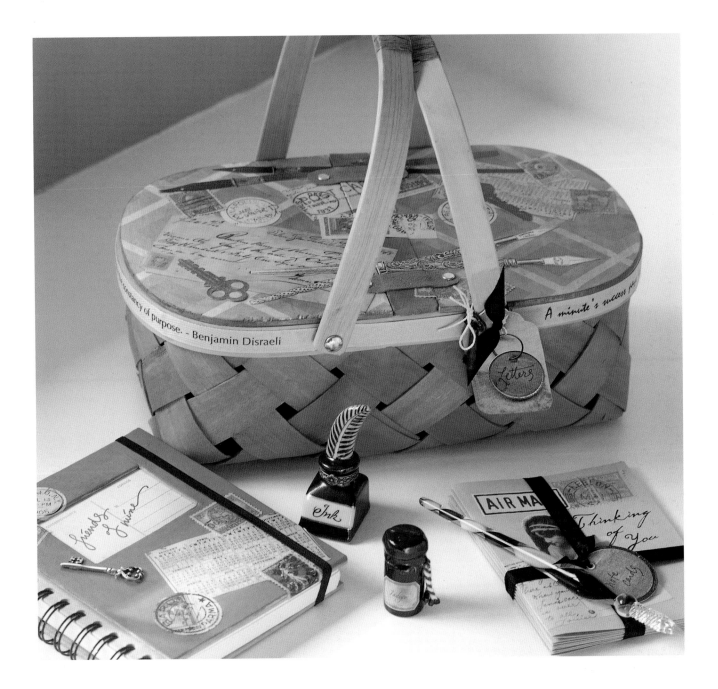

Finishing

Decoupaged and painted baskets can be protected with a varnish coating - properly protected, they will last for years. Be sure to include instructions for care if you are giving the piece as a gift.

To mix the varnish, roll - don't shake - the varnish container to minimize bubbles on your finished piece.

Pour the varnish in a small, disposable bowl to prevent the large container from being contaminated by dust or fibers. Use a large soft brush to slowly apply thin coats of varnish, and let each coat dry thoroughly before adding another. The more thin coats you apply, the finer the piece will appear.

For instant varnishing jobs, use clear varnish spray paint.

DECORATING WITH SILK FLOWERS

Silk flowers easily dress up a basket. To start, simply remove the flower heads and leaves from the stems (most silk flowers only need a good pull), or (easier still, and more economical) purchase flower heads or petals in the wedding departments of crafts and fabric stores. Then glue the flower pieces in place with a glue gun or fabric glue.

When applying the floral elements to the rim or front of a basket, it is best to start with a base. You can use moss and white glue or spray-on floral foam to create the base.

Forming a Base with Spanish Moss

This method provides a sturdy base and prevents the moss from shedding (falling apart) as the basket is used.

1. Place a large handful of moss on a piece of freezer paper or plastic sheeting.

2. Pour a good amount of thin-bodied white glue over the moss.

3. Use your hands (protected with disposable gloves) to pull the strands of the moss apart and mix in the glue. (photo 1) Keep pulling the moss apart until all the strands are coated with glue - it's a messy job, but will ensure that the moss forms a stiff base for decorative items.

4. Place the glue-dampened moss along the rim of the basket (photo 2) or wherever you wish to make your arrangement. Let dry.

5. *Option:* Use wire to secure the moss, wrapping the moss and the basket rim with 24-gauge wire.

6. Use hot glue to attach silk flowers and/or leaves. ❏

Photo 1. Mixing moss and white glue.

Photo 2. Placing the glue-dampened moss on the rim of a basket.

Photo 3. Applying spray-on floral foam.

Forming a Base with Spray-on Floral Foam

Spray-on foam, when set, acts as a very durable adhesive to hold an arrangement in place - no further wiring or gluing is needed. For best results, choose a color of foam to coordinate with the color of your basket or decorative items.

1. Protect your work area with freezer paper or a plastic sheet. Wear protective gloves when working with wet foam. Follow the foam manufacturer's instructions and prepare the canister with the nozzle.

2. Spray the top of the basket rim with foam. (photo 3)

3. Place the flower heads and leaves in the foam. (You will have about 20 minutes to work before the foam completely sets up.) ❏

NO-SEW FABRIC LINING

This glued-in lining that covers the inside of the basket is easy to do, and requires little fabric. You can use fabric glue instead of a glue gun if you wish.

Photo 1. Measuring the circumference.

Make the Side Lining Piece:

1. Measure the outside circumference of the basket and add 2". (Photo 1) Measure the depth of the basket and add 3". Using these measurements, cut a strip of fabric. TIP: Rather than buying many yards to make a strip for a large basket, cut shorter strips and sew them together to form one long strip. Add 1" per seam for the seam allowances.

2. Press the fabric. Turn under the top edge 1" and press. Turn under and press one end of the strip to form a finished end.

Make the Bottom Piece:

1. Measure the bottom of the basket and cut out a piece of mat board or stiff cardboard to fit.

2. Cut a piece of fabric 2" larger on all sides than the cardboard base.

3. Using a glue gun, cover the board with the fabric, folding over and gluing the corners first (photo 2), then the sides. Set aside.

Photo 2. Covering the cardboard for the bottom piece.

Photo 3. Gluing the side lining strip.

Install the Lining:

1. Using small plastic clamps or clothespins, attach the side lining to the inside of the basket. Check your measurements and determine where to start.

2. Remove the clamps and run a stream of hot glue around the rim, working in 4" sections, and adhere the lining. Use the clamps to hold the lining in place as you apply glue around the basket. (photo 3) Fold and pleat the corners as needed.

3. When the sides are lined and the glue has set, remove the clamps. Check for any spots that might need a little more glue.

4. Quickly apply a stream of hot glue to the bottom of the covered board and press into place. (photo 4) Keep

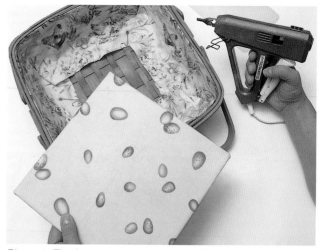

Photo 4. The bottom piece is ready to be glued in.

24

SEWN FABRIC LINING

This basket lining includes a decorative overhang - you make paper patterns for your basket, cut out the pieces, and sew them together. You can hold the lining in place with elastic cord or ribbon, which can be tied into a decorative bow. All seams are 1/2".

Make the Paper Patterns:

1. Place the basket on a piece of paper and trace around its base. Add 1/2" all the way around. Cut out the pattern. This is the bottom pattern.
2. Measure around the circumference of the basket at the widest point and add 1". Measure up the side of the basket and over the top. Add how long you wish the overhang to be plus 2". Using these measurements, create the side pattern.

Cut & Sew:

1. Pin the pattern pieces to the fabric. Cut out. (photo 1)
2. Fold the bottom piece into quarters and mark at the folds with pins. Fold the side piece into quarters and mark the quarters with pins.
3. Sew the ends of the side piece together, right sides together, creating a tube.
4. Match up the quarter marks on the side and bottom pieces and pin.
5. Sew the side piece to the bottom piece, right sides together, easing the fabric as you go.
6. Turn under the edge of the overhang to make a casing. Stitch.
7. Insert elastic cord or ribbon, using a bodkin. (photo 2)

Install:

Place the liner over the basket. (photo 3) ❑

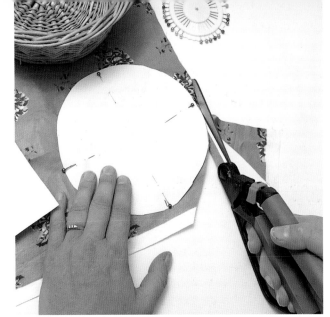

Photo 1. Cutting out the fabric.

Photo 2. Using a bodkin to insert elastic in the casing.

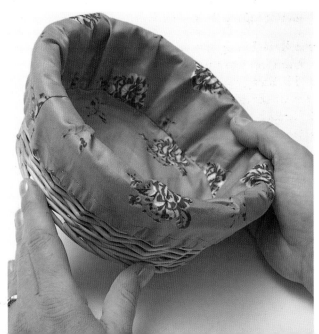

Photo 3. Placing the liner over the basket.

ADDING & DECORATING HANDLES

Adding a Handle

With strong wire or the stems from silk flowers, you can create and attach your own basket handles.

When constructing the handle, weave the handle pieces into the basket, all the way to the bottom. TIP: You may need to trim some basket weaves with wire cutters to fit the handle in.

After the handle is in place, use wire or natural raffia to secure it. For large baskets, it's a good idea to secure the handle at the top and bottom on each side. Test your handle by pulling on it - hard - to make sure it is firmly attached because you don't want it to come off when in

Photo 1. Forming a loop on the handle.

use. There is no such thing as a decorative handle that cannot be used - everyone automatically picks up a basket by its handle!

Wrapping a Handle

You can give a basket an additional decorative touch by wrapping the handle with twine or ribbon. There are several options - you can start at the base of the handle and, using a glue gun, completely cover the handle with ribbon. Or you can wrap part of the handle or only the part where the basket will be carried.

Here's a clever wrap without any knots showing. You'll need about 1 yard of twine per handle to make a wrap 3" to 4" wide.

Adding a handle with stems of artificial flowers.

1. With one end of the twine, form a loop on the top of the handle. (photo 1)

2. Start wrapping the handle from the opposite side of the loop, leaving the tail of the loop hanging out. Wrap the handle firmly and keep all the wraps pulled snug to the handle. (photo 2)

Photo 2. Wrapping a section of the handle.

Photo 3. Placing one end of the twine through the loop and pulling the other end.

3. When you have wrapped the amount you wish, thread the end of the twine through the loop and pull the exposed tail from the starting point. (The loop will pull the end of the twine into the wrap.) (photo 3)

4. Trim the exposed ends of the twine. (photo 4) ❏

Photo 4. Trimming the end of the twine.

MAKING BOWS

It is very easy to create beautiful bows when you know the techniques and use the wonderful ribbons that are found in craft and fabric stores. The gift basket industry uses an instant bow called a pull bow. The result is a perfect, big, beautiful bow that is created in the time it takes to pull two strings and gather the ribbon. (You can sometimes buy pull bows at craft and florist stores, though they are not widely available for retail sale.)

I've included instructions for making bows from narrow and wide ribbon on the pages that follow.

A multi-loop bow.

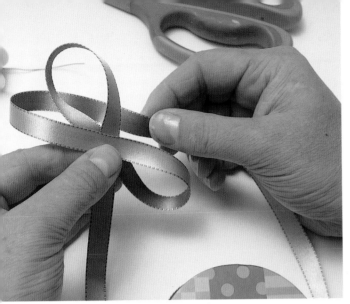

Photo 1. Forming the loops of the bow.

Multi-Loop Bow

This technique is generally used with narrower, soft ribbons. Satin ribbon, wire-edge ribbon, and cording all work with this method. When making this bow, work right from the ribbon spool so there is no cutting the ribbon too short or too long.

1. Leaving a piece for the tail, start the bow by forming a figure eight with the ribbon. Continue forming the loops on each side until you are satisfied with the fullness and the number of loops. (photo 1) You must have the same number of loops on each side so the ribbon ends at the center.

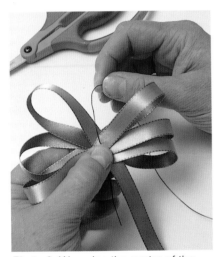

Photo 2. Wrapping the center of the bow with thin wire.

Photo 3. Twisting the ends of the wire to secure.

2. With 30-gauge wire, working right from the spool, secure the center of the bow with wire. (photo 2)

3. Grasp both ends of the wire at the back of the bow and twist the bow a few times to press the wires tightly against the bow. (photo 3) Trim the wires about 3" from the bow. (You can use the wire ends to attach the bow to the basket handle or to a larger bow for a layered look.)

4. To cover the wire in the middle of the bow and to add extra tails, tie a piece of ribbon at the center and knot. (photo 4) *Option:* Glue a button or other embellishment at the center of the bow.

5. Cut the tail ends at an angle and fluff the loops. ❑

Photo 4. Tying a piece of ribbon at the center to cover the wire.

Photo 1. Uncoiling paper ribbon.

Photo 2. Determining the size of the first set of loops.

Making a Paper Ribbon Bow

This is a great technique for making an inexpensive, beautiful large bow for your basket. This technique also can be used to make a bow with wide fabric ribbon. For this example, I've used coiled paper ribbon. You can purchase paper ribbon already uncoiled if you wish.

1. Gently open the paper ribbon coil and smooth out the ribbon. (photo 1)
2. To determine the size of the first set of loops, use the ribbon end as a gauge and make the loops double the ribbon width. (photo 2) (This basic measurement can be altered, but it works as a general rule for making the loops the right size relative to the width of the ribbon.)

Photo 3. Gathering the loops at the center.

3. Allow the loops to overlap slightly and trim the paper ribbon at the center. Place the loops on a hard surface and gather the loops at the center. (photo 3)
4. Wrap the center with 30-gauge wire, working right from the spool. Grasp the wire ends at the back of the bow and twist the bow a few times to press the wire tightly against the bow. (photo 4) **Do not cut** the wire.
5. Make another set of loops slightly larger than the first set. Gather at the center and place under the first set. Wrap with the wire and twist to secure. NOTE: At this point, add as many loop sets as you wish.

Photo 4. Securing the loops at the center with wire.

Photo 7. Trimming the ends in V-shapes.

Photo 5. Attaching the tails.

6. Cut a longer piece of paper ribbon for the tails, gather it at the center, and attach it below the loops with the wire. NOTE: Add as many tails as you wish. (photo 5) Cut the wire, leaving several inches attached to the bow.

7. For the center of the bow, cut a small piece of paper ribbon and loop it to form a tube. Gather it where the ends meet and secure with wire. (photo 6)

8. Use the wire to attach the center loop to the bow.

9. Trim the ends of the tails. For a V-shaped cut, fold the tail in half lengthwise and cut at an angle to the center fold. (photo 7)

10. Fluff the loops. Decorate the bow further by gluing dried or silk flowers or other embellishments. (photo 8) ❏

Photo 6. Making the center loop.

Photo 8. Embellishing a bow.

MAKING FABRIC RIBBON

This technique allows you to make a bow that exactly matches the lining of your basket by coating the leftover fabric from the lining with fabric stiffening glue. You can buy fabric stiffening glue or make your own by mixing white craft glue with water until it has the consistency of thick cream.

Be sure to protect your work surfaces with freezer paper or plastic sheeting. Wear a pair of disposable gloves to protect your hands while you make the ribbon.

Create a drying area for the ribbon by placing two wooden dowels between the backs of two chairs. Cover the dowels and the floor with freezer paper, shiny side up, or wax paper. Don't use newspaper on the dowels - the fabric will stick to it.

Pictured below: Fabric ribbons are used to decorate a seasonal basket.

1. Pour some fabric stiffening glue into a small pail or container. Dip a strip of fabric in the glue to saturate it. Squeeze out the excess by pulling the wet fabric through your hand as you lift the strip. (photo 1)

2. Hang the wet fabric over the dowels. (photo 2) Let dry overnight.

3. Remove the fabric from the drying rack and press with a hot, dry iron to remove the wrinkles. The fabric will be very stiff and the fibers will be fused together with glue.

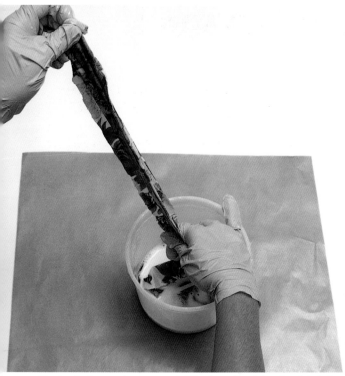

Photo 1. Squeezing excess stiffening glue from the fabric by pulling it through one gloved hand.

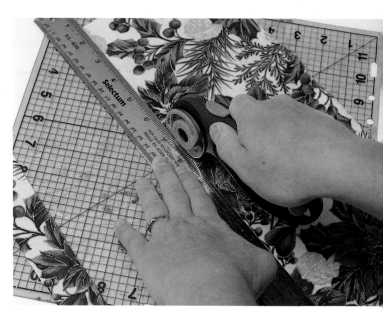

Photo 3. Cutting the stiffened fabric into strips to create the ribbon.

4. Use a cutting mat, ruler, and rotary cutter to cut your ribbon. Cut different widths to create a variety of ribbons. *Option:* Use decorative-edge scissors to create a scalloped or pinked edge on the ribbon. ❏

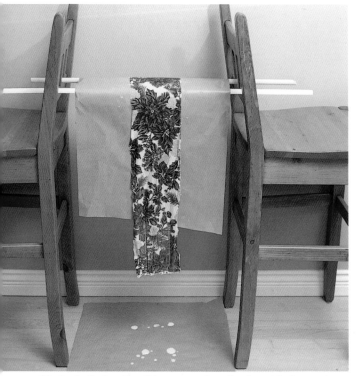

Photo 2. Drying the ribbon over dowels placed between two chairs. Freezer paper on the floor catches drips of stiffening glue.

TAGS & LABELS

When designing tags and labels, it's fun to extend the theme of the basket by incorporating materials you used to decorate the basket. It's a great way to create a professional coordinated look - and you can use up all those leftover bits and pieces! Example: Use a leftover piece of the lining fabric or fabric ribbon as the base for a tag.

Paper Tags

Paper tags are easy to make and can be accented with decorative stickers or lettering. A tag template with a cutting tool is great for cutting out lots of tags. When using lightweight paper for tags, glue the paper to a piece of heavier card paper to strengthen it and trim with decorative scissors.

Use ribbon, cord, or raffia to tie tags to the basket handle.

Polymer Clay Tags

Polymer clay is easy to work with. It comes in a wide range of colors and bakes in your home oven. Basic supplies for working with polymer clay include an acrylic roller, a polymer clay knife, and a ceramic tile to use as a work and baking surface.

When baked and allowed to cool, the clay can be sanded and drilled. Here's how to make a polymer clay tag:

1. Condition and warm the clay well, then roll out a thin sheet.
2. Use stamp alphabet sets and other textured tools to press designs in the clay sheet.
3. Follow the manufacturer's directions carefully for baking the clay tags in your oven.
4. Embellish further with paint or varnish. ❑

Embossed Metal Tags

Metal tags can be used for decorations or labels. Use 36- gauge metal sheets, available in aluminum, copper, or brass.

1. Cut out the tag from the metal sheeting, using metal shears.
2. Place the tag on a soft surface, such as a foam pad. Write on the metal with an embossing tool to lightly emboss the design on one side. (This side will be the front.)
3. Turn over the tag. Still on the foam pad, using the embossed lines as a guide, press firmly with the embossing tool to deepen the embossed design from the back.
4. Turn over again and bring out the embossed image by tracing around the embossed lines to create a clean, deep image.
5. *Option:* To antique, paint the tag with acrylic paint. Let dry, then sand the surface to reveal the embossed lettering. ❑

Recipe Cards

When you create a mix, be sure you give the same attention to providing instructions for use. You can print out your recipes on the computer and accent them with color graphics. Lots of beautiful blank and decorative self-adhesive labels are available to accent your packaged mixes - you can print on them with a computer printer.

A laminating machine can quickly laminate recipe cards for practical use in the kitchen - just punch a hole in one corner of the card and hang it on the basket or cellophane bag with gold cord.

If you're making lots of mixes for gifts, you can decorate the recipe cards with stickers or graphics and have them photocopied at a copy shop. To save money, gang up several recipes on one sheet.

RECIPE
Rose Petal Tea

Adding dried rose petals to a pot of plain tea makes a simple, but extraordinary fragrant blend. It also makes a refreshing iced tea. Each package makes one pot of tea.

Ingredients:
1 tablespoon dried rose petals (NOTE: **Only use** petals from roses that have not been sprayed.)
10 drops rose fragrance oil
4 tablespoons orange pekoe tea

Here's How:
1. Blend rose petals, rose fragrance oil, and tea.
2 Package in a cellophane bag. Top with a ...hing bow. ❑

RECIPE
Bean Soup Spice Mix

Makes four packages. Each is enough to flavor one jar of Bean Soup Mix.

Ingredients:
1 tablespoon salt
2 teaspoons ground black pepper
1 teaspoon chili powder
4 teaspoons cumin seed
4 tablespoons brown sugar
4 bay leaves

Here's How:
1. Mix all the ingredients except the bay leaves.
2. Divide into four equal portions.
3. Package each portion along with a bay leaf in a small zipper-top plastic bag. Attach the Bean Soup Recipe (see below) to the spice bag. ❑

RECIPE
Bean Soup Mix

Makes four jars, 2 cups each.

Ingredients:
1 cup navy beans
1 cup pinto beans
1 cup red kidney beans
1 cup yellow split peas
1 cup green split peas
1 cup brown lentils
1 cup red lentils
1 cup pearl barley

Here's How:
1. Combine the beans and barley in large bowl.
2. Measure 2 cups and place in a clean jar. Repeat to fill four jars. ❑

ASSEMBLING A GIFT BASKET
step-by-step

Here are the basic steps for constructing a gift basket. This photo series shows the Good Morning Sunshine Breakfast Basket. You'll find more information about what's in this basket in the section on Food Baskets.

Step 1 - Create a Base.

You need a base of fillers in the basket to raise the objects and anchor them in place. You can use floral foam blocks, brown paper, recycled paper shreds, newspaper, or a combination of fillers.

Trim the foam block to fit inside your basket, if needed. For larger baskets, you might have to cut blocks into several pieces and connect them with wooden skewers. Place the foam block in the basket and

Photo 2. Adding shreds and securing with wire.

surround it with paper fillers to keep it in place. TEST: You should be able to tip the basket upside down without the base falling out when you are finished.

Step 2 - Add Shreds and Wire.

You will add more shreds as you fill in the basket; this layer hides the base.

Add a layer of shreds over the base. Use pieces of 20-gauge wire bent into U-shapes to attach the shreds to the foam to ensure everything stays in place as you add the basket contents.

Photo 1. Packing a basket with a floral foam brick and shredded paper.

Photo 4. Placing a bottle in a "pocket."

Step 3 - Try Out Your Arrangement.

Design the basket like you would design a large bouquet of flowers, placing taller gift items in the back of the basket and smaller items toward the front.

Place the items in the basket to try out your arrangement before adhering or attaching anything. Distribute the weight of the gift items evenly to prevent the basket from tipping. Place larger items first, then smaller items.

Step 5 - Add Wooden Skewer Stakes and More Shreds.

Small items can be attached to wooden skewers and inserted in the foam block to create interest at different levels. Be sure to apply clear tape to the backs of paper packages before gluing on the skewers to prevent the packages from ripping when the skewer is removed.

continued on next page

Photo 3. Trying out an arrangement.

Step 4 - Create Pockets for Heavier Items.

Putting heavier items in pockets - hollows created in the shreds - helps the basket from becoming top heavy and tipping over and helps secure breakable items.

For heavier items, such as bottles, create small pockets in the shreds for the items. *Option:* Use glue dots to secure items to each other or to the basket.

Photo 5. Gluing wooden skewers to the backs of small items.

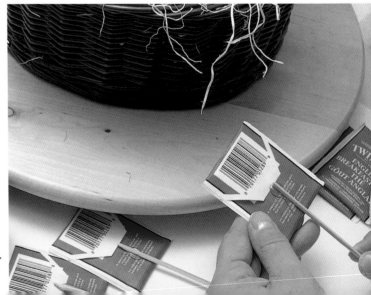

Assembling a Gift Basket, continued

Use hot glue to attach skewers on the backs of smaller items. Insert the skewers in the foam block for a secure hold. When all your items are secure in the container, fill the empty spaces with shreds. You can also add silk flowers, ivy picks, or other decorative items.

Step 6 - Wrap with Cellophane.

When you are pleased with your arrangement, it's time to wrap it with cellophane.

Cut a length of cellophane (or other wrapping material) three times the height of the container. Spread out the cellophane on a lazy susan or your work surface and place the basket in the center. Bring both ends of the cellophane together above the basket. Gather the sides of the cellophane in small pleats so it all meets in the middle above the basket. Use a twist tie to secure the gathered cellophane.

Photo 6. Wrapping with cellophane.

Step 7 - Taping the Openings.

Clear cellophane tape won't show. With clear cellophane tape, close any gaps or openings in the cellophane wrapping.

Photo 7. Taping the openings in the cellophane wrapping with clear cellophane tape.

Step 8 - Trimming the Top.

Cut at an angle to create a tapered end. Pull up the excess cellophane and trim about 6" from the twist tie. Fluff out the top piece of cellophane before adding the bow. (photo 8)

Photo 8. Trimming the cellophane with scissors.

Step 9 - Add the bow.

See instructions in this section for making bows. Construct your bow with a built-in tie or use the wire ends to attach it. Tie your beautiful handmade bow on the cellophane, covering the twist tie.

Photo 9 - Adding the bow.

The finished basket.

Gift
Basket
Projects

This section includes instructions for decorating and assembling more than two dozen gift baskets with a variety of themes and myriad occasions. For each project, you will find information about the type of basket used; the a list of decorations used for the basket and how to decorate it; a list of gift items placed in the basket; and instructions for assembling. Recipes and projects for the handcrafted items are included at the end of each project.

PLEASE NOTE: Although I have suggested wrapping most of the baskets in cellophane or tulle, the project photographs don't show the wrapping - if they did, the contents would be less clearly visible.

PERSONALIZED THEME BASKETS

As you create a gift basket, think about the person who will be receiving it. Because everyone has many hobbies and interests, finding one perfect gift for a person (or a group) may be difficult, but a gift basket based on a theme can be an easy way to create an ideal present. If you're not sure about the recipient's likes and dislikes or you don't know him or her well, do a little detective work to try to find out the person's interests and develop a personalized theme. TIP: Food items are enjoyed by almost everyone - just be aware of food preferences and special dietary considerations.

THINGS TO REMEMBER
when constructing a gift basket

- Package food items and scented items in separate baskets. *Never combine them* in the same basket - if you do, the food items will taste like soap.

- If you're including perishables in the basket, add a note on the outside with instructions to "Open me right away!"

- Don't place all the large, heavy items at the back of the basket - if you do, it could tip over.

- When arranging items, keep turning it around to view your arrangement from all sides to ensure a pleasing presentation.

- For a surprise basket - one where you want to hide the items from view - cover the basket with a few sheets of colorful tissue paper before wrapping with cellophane.

"OH, BABY!"
baby bath basket

This gift basket for a new baby holds a selection of bath items, toys, and a hooded towel to keep baby warm after the bath. The decorated, lined basket makes an attractive, practical storage container for the bath area. A plaid fabric in soft pastels - yellow, blue, pink, and lilac - is used to line a natural maize basket.

SUPPLIES

Basket:

Rectangular twined maize basket - 11" x 6" x 6" high

Basket Decorations:

• Fabric - 1/4 yd. of a soft, multi-colored plaid for lining

• Ribbon - 2 yds. yellow grosgrain, 3/8" wide; 2 yds. pink gingham, 3/8" wide; 2 yds. yellow gingham, 7/8" wide

• Polymer clay tag made with: pink polymer clay, alphabet stamps, blue acrylic paint

• Cellophane wrap

Gift Basket Contents:

• Brown kraft paper

• Pink pleated paper shreds

• Hooded bath towel (instructions follow)

• Bath toys

• Wash cloths

• Baby teddy soaps (instructions follow)

• Hairbrush and comb set

Other options: Baby shampoo, baby oil, baby powder, cotton swabs, cotton balls

continued on next page

continued from page 43

DECORATING THE BASKET

Make Lining:

1. Make a sewn lining, following the instructions in the Techniques section.

2. Thread yellow grosgrain ribbon through the casing. Set aside.

Make Tag:

1. Roll out conditioned pink polymer clay and trim to make a 3" x 1-1/2" tag.

2. Stamp "Oh Baby!" in the clay, using the alphabet stamps.

3. Use a plastic straw to make holes at each corner.

4. Bake according to the clay manufacturer's directions.

5. When cool, apply a wash of blue acrylic paint. Wipe away the excess paint to highlight the stamped details.

Install:

1. Use yellow grosgrain ribbon to attach the tag to the front of the basket, weaving the ribbon through the holes and tying it on the inside.

2. Place the liner inside the basket, tying the ribbon ends at the front in a bow.

ASSEMBLING THE GIFT BASKET

1. Tie the ribbons around the rolled up towel and face cloths.

2. Tie a piece of pink gingham ribbon around each soap. Place soaps in cellophane bags and tie the tops of the bags with ribbon.

3. Place the rolled up towel in the basket and stuff the basket bottom with brown paper. Top with pink pleated shreds.

4. Add the rest of the contents, arranging them so they face the front.

5. Using yellow gingham ribbon, make a multi-loop bow. Make a second multi-loop bow with pink gingham ribbon and attach to the yellow gingham bow. Glue a pastel yellow novelty star button to the center of the bow.

6. Wrap the basket in cellophane and attach the bow to the top. ❏

RECIPE

Gentle Teddy Soap

These cute soaps are a perfect welcome for a new baby. Chamomile fragrance is added for its gentle relaxation and calming effects. The recipe makes two bars.

Supplies:
6 ounces whitened glycerin soap base
1 teaspoon honey
8 drops chamomile fragrance oil
6 drops honey fragrance oil
2 drops yellow colorant
Teddy bear motif soap mold

Here's How:
1. Prepare the soap mold by rubbing the cavities with a thin film of petroleum jelly. Place the mold on wax paper and in an area that will not be disturbed while curing.
2. Melt the soap base in a microwave oven, following the manufacturer's directions.
3. Add the honey, fragrance oils, and colorant to the melted soap. Pour in the prepared molds.
4. Let the soap cool and cure for 30 minutes to 1 hour before releasing from the mold. ❏

PROJECT

Hooded Baby Towel

It takes only minutes to make this very practical gift. You'll need a thick, 100% cotton towel, a matching washcloth, and sewing thread.

1. Wash and dry the towel and washcloth.
2. Lay the towel on a flat surface. Place the washcloth on the top left-hand corner of the towel, pinning the two outer edges together.
3. Hand or machine stitch the two sides together. Fold up the bottom corner of the washcloth and press to form the hood. ❑

ROSE ROMANCE
wedding basket

This pretty basket is perfect for delivering a bread-and-jam breakfast to the bride's dressing room on the morning of the wedding. Tulle makes a wonderful, gauzy wrap for this basket and allows the steam of freshly baked croissants or muffins to escape. (A cellophane wrap could make things soggy.) The decorated basket could be used by the flower girl or to hold programs. It could also make a gorgeous Valentine's Day basket for a newlywed or engaged couple; the rose petal theme can be a nice hostess gift when invited out for tea. If you can't find rose petal tea and rose petal jelly, make them yourself with the recipes that follow.

SUPPLIES

Basket:

Oval wicker basket with handle, 12" x 8" x 13" high, painted white

Basket Decorations:

• 30 to 40 pink rose silk flower heads

• Acrylic craft paint - Cream

• Acrylic gel medium

• Embroidered napkin

• Tulle wrap

• 1-1/2" wide pink and white wire-edge ribbon

Gift Basket Gift Food Items:

• Fresh baked croissants *or* home-baked muffins or banana bread

• Rose Petal Jelly (instructions follow)

• Rose Petal Tea (instructions follow)

• *Nice Additions:* Victorian Rose Sugar (instructions follow), teacups with painted roses, rose motif napkins

CAUTION: When making food products that include roses, your homegrown roses are the best - **sprayed roses cannot be used**, and you cannot be 100% sure with roses from a florist. If using roses from a friend's garden, make absolutely sure no insecticides, fungicides, or other sprays were used.

DECORATING THE BASKET

1. Mix equal amounts of cream paint and gel medium to make a stain. Using a sponge, rub the basket with the stain mixture. Let dry before proceeding.

2. Using a glue gun, attach the rose heads to the entire base of the basket. Start from the bottom and attach the roses in rows. When you reach the top, place the roses so they overlap the rim of the basket slightly.

continued on page 48

HOME SWEET HOME
housewarming basket

Anyone who's just moved would love this basket. My sample has a green and purple color theme - for your basket, choose flower colors that match the recipient's decor. Lavishly decorated with silk flowers, the basket later can be used to hold magazines.

SUPPLIES

Basket:

Stained brown oval splint basket with two handles, 14" x 11" x 15" high

Basket Decorations:

• Silk flowers - A variety of large flower heads, flower sprays, and greenery

• 2 yds. sheer taupe ribbon, 3/4" wide

• 1 taupe tassel

• 1-1/2 yds. taupe trim, 3/4" wide

• Spray-on floral foam - Green *Option:* Make a base with Spanish moss and attach the flowers with hot glue.

Gift Basket Contents:

• Floral foam brick

• Brown kraft paper

• Pleated paper shreds

• Wooden skewers

• Roll of paper towels

• Rubber gloves

• Kitchen towels and sponges

• A book on cleaning or organizing

• Old-fashioned wooden clothespins

• Homemade cleaning products (instructions follow): Scented Home Misting Spray, Simmering Spice Potpourri, Carpet Sachet, Scented Cleaning Powder

DECORATING THE BASKET

1. Glue the trim around the rim of the basket with the cut ends at the front. If needed, cut the trim to fit around the handles, making sure you do not interfere with the handles' functioning. Use stop-fray glue to keep the cut ends from unraveling.

2. Place the basket on its side and support with an old rolled-up towel.

3. Spray floral foam on the front of the basket.

4. Arrange the silk flowers on the basket front, placing the larger flower heads first. Fill in with smaller blossom sprays and greenery. Add additional foam, if needed. Let the foam set up completely before moving.

ASSEMBLING THE GIFT BASKET

1. Place a brick of floral foam in the basket. (You may need two bricks if your basket is large.) Fill in around it with brown paper to create the base. Top with cream pleated paper shreds.

2. Place the contents in the basket, starting with the largest articles in the back.

Continued on page 53

Making the fragrant cleaning products is easy and economical, and they work beautifully.
They are environmentally safe, and fragrance oils make them a pleasure to use. Add the
fragrance oils directly to the products and mix well to incorporate the scents.
An alternative to the oval basket is a laundry basket. To fill the large space, use an upside-down
cleaning pail and add stuffing around it to hold the items in place.

RECIPE

Scented Home Misting Spray

Use this to freshen and scent linens or as a room air freshener. **Do not** *add colorants.*

Ingredients:
30 drops lemon fragrance oil
30 drops lavender fragrance oil
1 tablespoon vodka
1/2 cup distilled water

Here's How:
1. Mix the fragrance oils with the vodka.
2. Mix the alcohol-and-fragrance-oil blend with distilled water in a glass jar with a tight-fitting lid.
3. Shake every day for a week. (This helps the fragrances mellow and blend.)
4. Decant into a 4-ounce aluminum bottle with a fine mist spray nozzle.
5. Tie a piece of green raffia around the neck embellished with a miniature clothes peg. Use cream paper and newspaper print paper for the label. ❏

RECIPE

Simmering Spice Potpourri

Use this to create a welcoming spicy scent.

Ingredients:
1/2 cup cinnamon chips (Break cinnamon sticks into pieces with a pair of pliers.)
1/4 cup whole cloves
1/4 cup whole allspice berries
1/4 cup dried orange peel
To make your own: Cut orange peel into small pieces and place on a paper towel. Place in a warm place for 1 week. Make sure the peel is completely dry before using.
20 drops vanilla fragrance oil

Here's How:
1. Mix the ingredients well.
2. Package in an 8-ounce aluminum tin.
3. Label the tin with cream paper and newspaper print paper. Tie a piece of green raffia around the top. Embellish with a miniature clothes peg.

To use: Place 1 heaping tablespoon in a pot of simmering water. Add more water as needed. Discard after use. ❏

RECIPE

Scented Cleaning Powder

Use this powder to scrub tubs and sinks.

Ingredients:
1 cup baking soda
1/2 cup citric acid
1/2 cup borax
30 drops lemon fragrance oil
20 drops lavender fragrance oil

Here's How:
1. Mix the ingredients well.
2. Package the cleaning powder in a plastic bag and place in a small brown paper bag. (The mixture will solidify if not kept in the plastic bag.)
3. Label the bag with cream paper and newspaper print paper. Embellish with a miniature clothespin. Fold down the top of the bag and fasten with a wooden clothespin. ❏

RECIPE

Carpet Sachet

Carpet sachet can be sprinkled on a carpet, left for a few hours, and vacuumed up to expel odors and leave a fresh, clean scent.

Ingredients:
2 cups vermiculite (found in garden centers)
20 drops mango fragrance oil
10 drops lemon fragrance oil

Here's How:
1. Mix the oils with the vermiculite in a glass bowl or jar. Let rest for one day.
2. Package in a 16-ounce aluminum tin.
3. Label the tin with cream paper and newspaper print paper. Tie a piece of green raffia around the top of the tin. Embellish with a miniature clothes peg. ❏

Continued from page 50

3. Glue the wooden clothespins on wooden skewers and arrange in the basket, securing them into the floral foam brick.

4. Use taupe sheer ribbon to create a multi-loop bow. Glue a silk blossom at the center. Wire at the base of a handle at the top of the silk arrangement.

5. Loop the tassel on the handle so it hangs from the bow. ❑

WILD ABOUT YOU
thank you basket

This basket is decoupaged with animal print napkins and embellished with a beaded tassel and feather fringe trim. It's perfect for a corporate thank-you gift or a man's birthday. For the contents, search out shops in your area that showcase local food specialties and include a pair of salt and pepper grinders with cellophane bags full of sea salt and mixed peppercorns. (You'll be surprised how many items can be fitted in a small basket.) Later, the basket can hold mail at the office or at home.

SUPPLIES

Basket:

Wooden splint basket with handle, 9" x 9" x 12" high

Basket Decorations:
- Black acrylic paint
- Animal print paper napkins
- Decoupage medium
- 30" feathered trim
- Imitation natural colored raffia (to wrap the handle)
- Decorative buttons to match theme, shanks removed
- Beads and black jute tassel
- Cellophane wrap

Gift Basket Contents:
- Local food items
- Crackers, removed from their original box and placed in cellophane bags
- Salt and pepper grinders with cellophane bags of peppercorns and sea salt
- Recycled paper shreds
- Excelsior

DECORATING THE BASKET

1. Paint the handle black. Let dry.
2. Following the decoupage instructions in the Techniques section, decoupage the napkins to the basket, overlapping them to cover the inside rim. Let dry completely.
3. With raffia, wrap the top of the handle. Glue decorative buttons to the handle at the ends of the raffia wrap.
4. Glue the feather fringe around basket rim. Cut as necessary so the handle mechanics are not impaired. Use stop-fray glue on the cut ends.
5. Make a small tassel with black jute cord and add beads. Tie the tassel around the handle.

ASSEMBLING THE GIFT BASKET

1. Since the bag of sea salt is not very attractive, place it in the bottom of the basket with recycled paper shreds to fill the space and create the base. Cover the base with excelsior.
2. Arrange the contents, making indentions in the shreds to secure the heavy items. Make sure the weight is balanced so the basket won't tip over.
3. *Optional:* Wrap with cellophane and top with a natural raffia bow. ❑

FLORAL GOOD WISHES
plant basket

A simple, inexpensive basket was colored and decorated with flower blossoms and leaves around the rim. It creates a beautiful basket for presenting a potted plant or a single item such as a bottle of wine. The basket can be used for displaying the plant or as a charming wastebasket.

SUPPLIES

Basket:

Natural wicker round basket, 8" diameter x 7" high

Basket Decorations:

• Pale green spray paint
• 40 to 50 silk hydrangea blossoms, 1-1/2" to 2-1/2" diameter, removed from stems
• Silk leaves removed from stems
• Hot glue and gun

Gift Basket Contents:

• A potted plant
• Plastic sheeting
• Paper shreds

DECORATING THE BASKET

1. Spray basket with two coats of paint. Let dry completely.

2. Using a glue gun, attach the leaves at the bottom of the basket's rim, overlapping the leaves as you go.

3. Glue the flower blossoms around the top of the rim, overlapping to the inside of the basket for full coverage.

ASSEMBLING THE GIFT BASKET

1. Cut a piece of plastic sheeting 12" in diameter. Place under and around the pot and secure with a rubber band. Place plant in basket. (The plant can be watered without the leaking through and soaking the stuffing and the basket.)

2. *Optional:* To lift the pot so the top is even with the basket rim, add recycled paper shreds to the bottom of the basket.

3. Place shreds around the pot to keep it secure in the basket for transporting. ❑

JUST WHAT
THE DOCTOR ORDERED
get well basket

*This basket is brimming with soothing and comforting articles
when someone is not feeling well - the packages were glued to
wooden skewers to form a "get well" bouquet. The decorated basket
is perfect to hold items or fruit in a country kitchen.
The "chicken soup" lining is a wonderful surprise for the recipient
when all the gift items are removed. I used a purchased package of
chicken soup for the sample basket, but it's more fun to create your
own soup using the recipe that follows.*

TIDINGS OF COMFORT & JOY
christmas basket

This basket holds gifts and displays them decoratively - it's lined with a seasonal-print fabric and filled with bags of firestarters to be given as gifts to folks who drop by during the holiday season. Alternately, you could fill the basket with bags of homemade caramel popcorn mix, bags of Christmas cookies, or jars of homemade preserves.

Fresh greenery is used as a fragrant filler and to create the base to hold the gift bags.

SUPPLIES

Basket:

Natural splint basket with side
  handles, 12" x 10" x 6" high

Basket Decorations:

• Christmas fabric for lining in two
  coordinating prints (I used a
  poinsettia print for the sides and a
  smaller scale burgundy print for
  the bottom.)

• Bow made from burgundy print
  fabric (See the instructions for
  making fabric ribbon bows in the
  Techniques section.)

• 1-1/4 yds. burgundy trim

• Burgundy tassel

Gift Basket Contents:

• Handmade fire starters (instructions follow), packaged in
  cellophane bags with gold dots
  and gold twist ties

• Fresh evergreen

PROJECT

Pine Cone Fire Starters

Use these fragrant waxed cones for decoration and to quickly start a blaze in the fireplace.

Supplies:
Paraffin wax
Candle dye *or* old crayon pieces
Candle fragrance
Candlewicking
Pine cones

Here's How:
1. Melt the paraffin wax in a double boiler. Add candle dye or crayons and candle fragrance to the melted wax.
2. Tie a 12" piece of candlewicking around the base of a pine cone. Tie the other end of the candlewicking to another cone. (You now have two cones connected with a piece of wick.)
3. Dip the cones one by one in the melted wax until you are happy with the coverage.
4. Hang the cones to dry over a yardstick propped between two chairs after covering the floor with newspaper to catch any drips. Let dry.
5. Trim the wick so there is a 2" fuse on each cone.

To use: Display your fragrant cones in a basket by the fireplace far enough away so no sparks ignite them. To quickly start a fire, place one cone in the fireplace and light the wick. ❏

DECORATING THE BASKET

1. Measure, cut, and line the basket, following the step-by-step instructions for a no-sew liner in the Techniques section.

2. Attach the burgundy trim around the top rim of the basket, using a glue gun.

3. Tie a tassel to the handle. Affix the fabric bow to the basket over the tassel with the wire ends.

ASSEMBLING THE GIFT BASKET

1. Fill the basket with fresh evergreens.

2. Place the filled cellophane bags on top. Display the basket in your front entrance, ready for holiday guests. ❏

FOOD BASKETS

Storage Tips

When you create your own food baskets, you can make and package the mixes yourself and even include fresh ingredients - but if you use fresh items in your gift basket, be sure to attach a notice that the basket needs to be opened right away.

One excellent quality of your homemade mixes is that they are void of preservatives. It is best to label homemade mixes with a "best-before" date for maximum freshness. Even though many mixes would last much longer than suggested, the colors and flavors will fade.

Here are my suggested best-before dates for various types of mixes:

- Dressing, dip, and seasoning blends - 6 months

- Beans, dried vegetable soup blends - 3 months

- Bread, muffin, and scone mixes - 2 weeks in refrigerator

- Cookie and cake mixes - 2 months; with nuts - 1 month

- Coffee and tea mixes - 3 months

Food Basket Ideas

In this section, you'll see several ideas for food baskets. Here are more:

French Picnic Basket - Pate, cheeses, crackers, wine, cookies, plastic wine glasses, paper plates, plastic cutlery.

Cookie Monster Basket - Cookie mix, chocolate chips, nuts, sprinkles, cookie cutters, wooden spoon, cookie sheet.

Nut Lovers Basket - Bags of roasted nuts, fresh nuts in the shell, chocolate covered nuts, nut crackers.

Texas Chili Basket - Chili mix, cornbread mix, jar of homemade salsa, iced tea.

Tea Basket - Tea, tea biscuits, sugar cubes, lemon, lace-edged napkins, canned cakes, tea ball, teacups and saucers.

Coffee Basket - Coffee, flavored coffee syrups, chocolate covered coffee beans, chocolate dipped spoons, biscotti, coffee mugs.

Chocolate Lovers Basket - Chocolate covered pretzels, chocolate truffles, chocolate syrup - anything with chocolate!

Fresh Fruit & Cheese Basket - Seasonal fruits, gourmet cheeses.

Indian Curry Basket - Curry paste, jasmine rice, garlic, green chili paste, mango chutney.

Snacks Basket - Popcorn seasoning blends, cookie mixes, chip dip mixes.

Healthy Snacks Basket - Low salt chips, popcorn, salsa, dried fruit, fruit leather, energy drink, nuts.

Pizza Basket - Pizza dough mix, Italian seasoning, pizza sauce, stick of pepperoni, grated cheese, pizza pan, pizza cutter.

Barbecue Basket - Barbecue sauce, spiced rubs, oven mitts, apron, barbecue utensils.

TUSCAN SUN
meal-in-a-basket

This basket contains a complete Italian feast. It's perfect for welcoming folks to a new home or as a hostess gift. Instructions follow on the next page.

SUPPLIES

Basket:

Acorn-shaped wicker trug basket with splint handle, 14" x 9" x 10" high

Basket Decorations:

- Acrylic craft paint - Black plum
- Acrylic gel medium
- Sponge
- Silk olive branches with artificial olives
- Spanish moss and white glue
- 20-gauge wire
- Oval label frame with brown paper label
- Cellophane wrap
- Raffia

Gift Basket Contents:

- Floral foam brick
- Brown kraft paper
- Excelsior
- Italian bread
- Pasta
- Sauce ingredients - Fresh herbs (oregano, basil, rosemary, thyme), tomato sauce, olive oil, garlic, artichoke hearts
- Parmesan or Romano cheese
- *Other Options:* Bread sticks, jar of roasted peppers, olives, can of anchovies, a bottle of red wine

DECORATING THE BASKET

1. Mix equal amounts black plum paint and gel medium to make a stain. Stain the basket and handle, using a sponge. Wipe off the excess to give the basket an antique look.

2. Create a base around the rim with Spanish moss and white glue, following the instructions in the Techniques section. Let dry.

3. Secure the base to the rim with 20-gauge wire.

4. Decorate the rim with small sprigs of silk olive leaves, attaching them with a glue gun.

5. Embellish the basket with the oval label frame glued in place with metal glue. Use the photo as a guide for placement.

ASSEMBLING THE GIFT BASKET

1. Create a base with a brick of floral foam and brown paper. Top with natural excelsior.

2. Arrange the items in the basket.

3. Wrap the basket with cellophane.

4. Top with a raffia bow. ❏

GOOD MORNING, SUNSHINE
breakfast basket

Invited to the country for the weekend? Bring breakfast! This bountiful basket holds everything you need to make a delicious breakfast feast for a crowd. Yellow and green are a cheery color combination.

SUPPLIES

Basket:

Round wicker basket, 11" diameter
  x 4" high

Basket Decorations:

• Green spray paint

• Green paper ribbon

• Natural raffia

• Large silk sunflower

• Cellophane wrap

Gift Basket Contents:

• Floral foam brick

• Recycled paper shreds

• Natural excelsior

• Jam and fresh bread

• Pancake mix and maple syrup

• Homemade Granola (recipe
  follows)

• Coffee and tea

• *Nice Additions:* Fresh fruit
  (bananas, oranges, or a basket of
  fresh berries)

ASSEMBLING THE GIFT BASKET

1. Place a brick of floral foam in the basket. Secure with
   recycled paper shreds. Top with natural excelsior.

2. Arrange the items in the basket.

3. Wrap the basket with cellophane.

4. Make a large bow from paper ribbon and raffia. Attach
   the sunflower at the center. Wire bow to basket. ❑

RECIPE
Homemade Granola
Makes 5 cups (10 servings, 1/2 cup each).

Ingredients:
2 cups rolled oats (*not* instant)
1 cup shredded coconut
1/2 cup chopped almonds
1/2 cup chopped hazelnuts
1/2 cup wheat germ
2 tablespoons brown sugar
1/2 teaspoon cinnamon
1/2 cup honey
1/4 cup oil
1 cup dried fruit (cranberries, chopped apricots, dried apples,
  and/or dates)

Here's How:
1. Combine oats, coconut, nuts, wheat germ, brown sugar, and
   cinnamon.
2. Combine honey and oil. Stir into mixture.
3. Spread in a 9" x 13" baking pan.
4. Place in a 300-degree oven and bake 40 to 50 minutes until light
   golden brown, stirring every 15 minutes. Remove from oven.
5. Stir in dried fruit. Place in another pan and let cool.
6. Package in cellophane bags. ❑

SEASONED WITH LOVE
meal-in-a-basket

Bean soup is a favorite comfort food for many people, and this basket contains ingredients and spices to make a lip-smacking dish. The spices are packaged separately to preserve their freshness. Kitchen utensils round out the presentation. Gilded silk leaves are soft metallic accents.

SUPPLIES

Basket:

Rectangular natural willow basket, handle removed,
10" x 8" x 4" high

Basket Decorations:

• Silk oak leaves in fall colors

• Artificial acorns

• Spray adhesive

• Variegated gold leafing

• Spray-on floral foam

• 24" length of 1/4" copper pipe

• 20-gauge copper wire

• Embossed copper tag

• Natural-colored paper ribbon

• Cellophane wrap

Gift Basket Contents:

• Brown kraft paper

• Wood skewers

• Jar of Bean Soup Mix (recipe follows)

• Bean Soup Spice Mix (recipe follows)

• Can of tomatoes, lemon, garlic, pepper sauce

• Loaf of bread

• Wooden spoon, measuring spoons

DECORATING THE BASKET

1. Bend the copper pipe into a U-shape that fits the length of the basket and forms a handle. Push the ends of the pipe into the basket, weaving them into the willow. (You may need to cut out some of the willow pieces so the handles will fit.) Use copper wire to securely fasten the handle to the basket.

2. Gild 16 to 18 silk leaves by spraying them with adhesive and applying metallic leafing. Brush off the excess leafing with a soft brush.

3. Create a base around the rim of the basket with spray-on floral foam. Insert both gilded and un-gilded leaves

RECIPE

Bean Soup Mix

Makes four jars, 2 cups each.

Ingredients:
1 cup navy beans
1 cup pinto beans
1 cup red kidney beans
1 cup yellow split peas
1 cup green split peas
1 cup brown lentils
1 cup red lentils
1 cup pearl barley

Here's How:
1. Combine the beans and barley in large bowl.
2. Measure 2 cups and place in a clean jar. Repeat to fill four jars. ❑

RECIPE

Bean Soup Spice Mix

Makes four packages. Each is enough to flavor one jar of Bean Soup Mix.

Ingredients:
1 tablespoon salt
2 teaspoons ground black pepper
1 teaspoon chili powder
4 teaspoons cumin seed
4 tablespoons brown sugar
4 bay leaves

Here's How:
1. Mix all the ingredients except the bay leaves.
2. Divide into four equal portions.
3. Package each portion along with a bay leaf in a small zipper-top plastic bag. Attach the Bean Soup Recipe to the spice bag. ❑

around the rim. As the foam starts to firm up, add the acorns to the rim arrangement as accents.

4. Coil small pieces of copper wire around a pencil. Add the curly tendrils to the silk leaf arrangement and place them around the base of the handle.

RECIPE

Bean Soup Recipe

Attach this recipe to each package of Bean Soup Spice Mix.

Ingredients:

1 jar Bean Soup Mix
2 quarts water
1 large onion, chopped fine
1 clove garlic, minced

1 package Bean Soup Spice Mix
1 ham hock
1 can tomatoes
Juice of 1/2 lemon

Here's How:

1. Rinse bean mix. Place in large bowl and cover with water. Soak overnight.
2. Drain beans and rinse in cold water.
3. Place 2 quarts water, soaked beans, ham hock, and spice mix in a large pot. Cover and bring to a boil. Reduce heat and simmer for two hours until beans are tender.
4. Add lemon, garlic, tomatoes, and onion. Simmer 30 minutes more, stirring occasionally.
5. Remove ham hock from soup. Cut meat off bone and add to soup.

To serve: Add a splash of pepper sauce. Serve with fresh bread. ❑

ASSEMBLING THE GIFT BASKET

1. Create a base with brown paper.
2. Place the bean soup mix in a center pocket. Arrange the other items around the jar.
3. Stake the loaf of bread on a wooden skewer and push the skewer into the willow basket.
4. Wrap with cellophane.
5. Make a bow with natural paper ribbon. Accent with an acorn. ❑

STYLISH SUSHI
food basket

This food basket, packaged in a decorated bamboo steamer, contains supplies for making sushi - the recipient just adds the fish or vegetables. The basket is a terrific kitchen storage container; because it was glued and painted, it can't be used for steaming foods.

SUPPLIES

Basket:

Chinese steamer basket (found at Asian groceries, import stores, and kitchen shops)

Basket Decorations:

- Brown spray paint, gloss
- Decoupage medium
- Handmade papers, some with printed Chinese characters
- Beaded black tassel
- Black cord
- Cellophane wrap

Gift Basket Contents:

- Floral foam brick
- Brown kraft paper
- Natural excelsior
- Wooden skewers
- Sushi supplies - Cellophane bag of sushi rice, dried sheets of nori seaweed, a tube of wasabi, a bottle of soy sauce, a bamboo mat
- *Nice Additions:* A recipe book on making sushi, a rice paddle, chopsticks, rice vinegar, a jar of pickled ginger

DECORATING THE BASKET

1. Using pliers, remove the bamboo racks in each steamer section. Glue the steamer sections together with strong white craft glue. Set aside to dry completely.
2. Spray paint the outside of the basket and the lid with glossy dark brown paint. Let dry.
3. Tear the handmade paper into strips as wide as the sections of the steamer. Decoupage the paper strips on the sides of the basket. See the Techniques section for decoupage instructions.
4. Cut out a variety of square Chinese characters. Decoupage the cutouts on top of the paper strips.
5. Tie a black tassel adorned with beads to the handle on the lid.

ASSEMBLING THE GIFT BASKET

1. Make a base with a brick of floral foam and brown kraft paper. Top the base with natural excelsior.
2. Using the photo as a guide, place the lid in the basket and secure with wooden skewers from the back. (They will hold the lid in place without glue.)
3. Arrange the items in front of the lid.
4. Wrap the basket in cellophane. Tie with black cord. ❑

MOVIE MADNESS
treat basket

A gift basket filled with treats and a favorite movie wishes the recipient an evening of fun - it's a great presentation for a favorite babysitter or a young family. The beads wired to the basket create a sparkling display piece that will be enjoyed long after the treats are gone.

SUPPLIES

Basket:

Antique brown round wicker tray,
   10" diameter, 3" tall (without
   added handles)

Basket Decorations:

• Glass beads - Green, purple

• 20-gauge wire - Green, purple

• 16-gauge brown floral wire

• Polymer clay and bead tag

• Sheer purple ribbon

• Cellophane wrap

Gift Basket Contents:

• Brown paper

• Cream pleated paper shreds

• Caramel Popcorn (recipe follows)

• Sugar & Spice Nuts (recipe follows)

• Movie video

• Candy and individual packages of microwave
  popcorn wrapped with coordinating paper

RECIPE

Caramel Popcorn

Ingredients:
2 cups sugar
2 cups light brown sugar, firmly packed
2 cups light cream
1 teaspoon soft butter
3/4 teaspoon vanilla
1/4 cup whole almonds
1/4 cup whole pecans
6 cups popped popcorn, all unpopped kernels removed

Here's How:
1. In a heavy saucepan, combine sugars and cream and stir until sugar is dissolved. Boil, uncovered, without stirring until syrup reaches the soft-ball stage (235 to 240 degrees F.)
2. Cool for 10 minutes. Beat with a wooden spoon until thickened.
3. Add vanilla, nuts, and popcorn and mix well.
4. Pour on sheets of parchment paper to cool.
5. Break apart larger pieces before packaging in a cellophane bag. ❏

DECORATING THE BASKET

Make the Handle:

1. Cut 16-gauge wire into four 24" lengths.

2. Twist together two pieces and attach to the basket by coiling the ends around the rim. Twist the remaining two pieces together and attach the ends in the same manner.

3. Cut a 12" piece of wire and wrap it around the two handles at the top. Trim excess wire and make sure the sharp ends are tucked in to prevent injury.

Decorate the Rim:

The beads are threaded on 20-gauge wire and wrapped around the rim.

1. Attach the end of the purple wire to the base of the handle. Thread on three large beads and two smaller beads and wrap the wire around the rim. Continue to thread on the beads and wrap the wire around the rim until you have gone all the way around the basket. Twist the wire ends to secure.

2. Use the same technique with the green wire, three large green beads, and two smaller purple beads, wrapping and beading around the entire basket rim.

Make & Attach the Tag:

See the Techniques section for information about making polymer clay tags.

1. Make a tag from purple polymer clay. Make a hole in one end and stamp with the word "enjoy."

2. Bake according to the clay manufacturer's instructions.

3. Brush with green acrylic paint to accent the lettering. Let dry.

4. Apply a gloss varnish finish. Let dry.

5. Thread a piece of wire through the hole and thread on beads to accent. Use the wire ends to attach the tag to the top of the handle.

ASSEMBLING THE GIFT BASKET

1. Create a base with brown paper. Top with cream pleated paper shreds.

2. Attach a multi-loop bow made from sheer ribbon to the top of the handle.

3. Wrap with cellophane. ❑

RECIPE
Sugar & Spice Nuts
I used pecans, but you could use other nuts.

Ingredients:
1/2 cup brown sugar
1/2 cup sugar
1 teaspoon cinnamon
1/2 teaspoon ginger
1/2 teaspoon nutmeg
1 egg white
1 tablespoon water
1 teaspoon vanilla
4 cups pecans

Here's How:
1. In a bowl, combine sugars and spices.
2. In a small bowl, beat the egg white with the water until frothy. Add to sugar and spice mixture.
3. Stir in nuts.
4. Spread on a greased baking sheet. Bake at 325 degrees F. for 20 minutes, stirring occasionally, until dry looking and slightly browned. ❑

FRESH-AS-A-DAISY
bath basket

This daisy fresh collection is packaged in soft yellows and creams. Floral and mint fragrances come together in a stimulating, refreshing collection of pampering gifts that you make yourself. The decorated seagrass basket includes all parts of the silk daisies - flower heads, leaves, and stems - to create this cheerful arrangement.

PAMPERING SPA
bath basket

Calming, relaxing blues and balanced, tranquil greens color this spa-inspired pampering basket. The lined basket holds a collection of handmade bath products and natural bath items that provide a wonderful way to relax and refresh with heavenly aromas.

continued from page 86

SUPPLIES

Basket:

Low, rectangular coiled maize basket with side handles, 14" x 10" x 7" high

Basket Decorations:

• Green and blue checked fabric

• Two-tone blue and green satin ribbon, 1/2" wide

• Natural raffia

• Cellophane wrap

Gift Basket Contents:

• Brown kraft paper

• Natural excelsior

• Handmade spa products - Refreshing Salt Rub, Spa Salts, Spa Therapy Soap, Massaging Marbles (instructions follow)

• *Nice Additions:* A fragrant candle, sea sponge, exfoliating gloves, bath scrubbers, massage balls, net sponges

DECORATING THE BASKET

1. Measure, cut and sew the lining, following the instructions for a sewn lining in the Techniques section. To accommodate the handles, cut a shallow U-shape around them in the side lining piece.

2. Insert the two-toned satin ribbon into the casing. Tie under the handles in a bow.

ASSEMBLING THE GIFT BASKET

1. Make a base of crumpled brown kraft paper and top with natural wood excelsior.

2. Arrange the gifts in the basket.

3. Wrap with cellophane. Top with a natural raffia bow. ❏

PROJECT

Spa Bath Salts

The legendary allure of a fragrant, relaxing bath is created with these perfumed salts, which contain glycerin for extra moisturizing. The recipe makes one jar of salts but can be easily doubled or tripled.

Supplies:

1 cup chunky sea salt
1 tablespoon glycerin
Soap Colorants - Blue, green
10 drops tangerine fragrance oil
5 drops lime fragrance oil
5 drops peppermint fragrance oil

Here's How:

1. Divide the salt into three glass jars and add:
   To Jar 1 - 3 to 4 drops blue colorant, 5 drops peppermint fragrance oil, 1 teaspoon glycerin
   To Jar 2 - 3 to 4 drops green colorant, 5 drops lime fragrance oil, 1 teaspoon glycerin
   To Jar 3 - 10 drops tangerine fragrance oil, 1 teaspoon glycerin
2. Place lids on the jars. Shake well to distribute the color and fragrance. Allow to stand one day.

To package: Mix the salts together and pack in an 8-ounce glass jar. Top the jar with a circle of brown paper, a piece of natural raffia, and a tag.

To use: Draw a warm bath and add the fragrant salts to the running water. Hop in and relax, inhaling deeply to experience the refreshing and soothing aromas. ❏

— PROJECT —

Spa Therapy Soap

This healing soap's invigorating scents help rejuvenate and restore your healthy glow. Makes two bars.

Ingredients:

8 ounces white glycerin soap base
4 ounces clear glycerin soap base
20 drops peppermint fragrance oil

30 drops lime fragrance oil
Two 4-ounce rectangular soap molds
Blue and green soap colorants

Here's How:

1. Melt 4 ounces of whitened glycerin soap base in a microwave oven according to the soap base manufacturer's instructions. Mix in the peppermint fragrance oil and 4 drops blue colorant. Pour in one mold.
2. Melt the remaining 4 ounces of whitened glycerin soap base in the microwave. Add the lime fragrance oil and 4 drops green colorant. Pour in the other soap mold. Leave to solidify, approximately 1/2 hour.
3. Unmold the blue and green soap bars. Cut into 1" x 1/2" rectangular chunks. Place in freezer to chill.
4. Melt the clear glycerin soap base in the microwave and add 3 drops blue colorant.
5. Place the chilled soap chunks, mixing up the colors, in the two molds. Pour the clear glycerin base over the chilled soap chunks and let set. When the soap has hardened, unmold.

To package: Wrap the soaps tightly with plastic wrap. Tie a piece of satin ribbon around each soap. Add a tag. ❏

— PROJECT —

Refreshing Salt Rub

Rub these salts on your skin while you stand in the tub before a cleansing shower. The glycerin moisturizes while the salt tones and exfoliates the skin.

Supplies:

1 cup epsom salts
1 cup sea salt
1 tablespoon glycerin
15 drops peppermint fragrance oil
10 drops lime fragrance oil

Here's How:

1. Mix all the ingredients well.
2. Package in a clear glass jar. ❏

— PROJECT —

Massaging Marbles

A foot bath with marbles is a truly relaxing and pampering way to de-stress after a busy day. Include a plastic net bag of marbles in the gift basket with these instructions:

Place 1/4 cup of Spa Salts and the marbles in a warm footbath. Gently rub your feet against the marbles for a stimulating massage. NOTE: Do not put the marbles in the bathtub - that would create a dangerous, unstable surface. ❏

LIFE'S A BEACH
bon voyage basket

This basket is a great send-off gift for someone leaving on a tropical journey or for someone who needs some restful time at the beach. The decorated basket can be used to hold rolled towels in the bathroom after the trip - it's very sturdy and will hold up under a lot of use.

SUPPLIES

Basket:
Natural bleached willow basket with handle, 13" x 9" x 14" high

Basket Decorations:
• Spray paints - Teal, light green
• Spanish moss
• Silk olive leaves
• Sea shells
• 20-gauge blue wire
• Dried starfish
• Sea glass
• Natural raffia
• Cellophane wrap

Gift Basket Contents:
• Brown kraft paper
• Green pleated paper shreds
• Beach towel
• Sunscreen
• Suntan lotion
• A novel
• Snacks and a water bottle
• *Nice Additions:* A Frisbee® toy, sunglasses, a pail and a shovel

continued on next page

DECORATING THE BASKET

1. Basecoat the entire basket, inside and out, with light green spray paint. Let dry.
2. Spray the top and handle of the basket with teal paint to create a shaded, two-toned effect.
3. Create a base for the silk olive leaves along two sides of the basket with Spanish moss and white glue. (See the Techniques section for instructions.) Set aside to dry.
4. Drill a small hole in each shell. To do this safely and not break the shells, wear safety goggles, work on a wooden board, and use a small drill bit on a rotary type drill. To hold the shell in place while you drill, place the shell on some plasticine clay, which will support the shell to prevent breakage.
5. Attach the shells to the rim of the basket with wire. (The wire also helps hold the moss in place.) Start with larger shells at the base of the handle and work out to the sides with smaller shells.
6. Using a glue gun, add the dried starfish and sea glass.
7. Add a bunch of raffia to the arrangement by making a knot in the middle of some raffia strands, bending them, and gluing them in place.

ASSEMBLING THE GIFT BASKET

1. Place the rolled up towel in the basket. Secure with brown paper. Add pleated green paper shreds.
2. Place the remaining items in the basket.
3. Wrap with cellophane. Top with a raffia bow with shells glued at the center. ❑

NEEDLE LITTLE LOVE
Knitting Basket

This contemporary black, white, and yellow basket holds the tools and supplies to get started with knitting. The basket is attractive enough to place on a shelf or side table ready to knit. If the recipient is a beginner, don't forget to add a book on knitting or a coupon offering lessons.

Instructions begin on page 95.

93

continued from page 93

SUPPLIES

Basket:

Splint square tapered basket, 9" x 9" x 7"

Basket Decorations:
- Glossy black spray paint
- 1-1/4 yards black and white trim
- 1/4 yard black and white checked fabric for lining
- Mat board
- Gold label frame
- Black ribbon with white polka dots
- Yellow button
- Cellophane wrap

Gift Basket Contents:
- Brown kraft paper
- Skeins of colored wool (cover the labels with black and white ribbon)
- Bamboo knitting needles
- Beginner's knitting book
- Scissors

DECORATING THE BASKET

1. Spray the entire basket with black paint, inside and out. Let dry.
2. Measure and cut the fabric and line the basket according to the instructions for the no-sew lining in the Techniques section. Glue the trim around the inside top edge of the basket before adding the side lining piece.
3. Using metal glue, attach the gold label frame to the front of the basket. Add a paper label to describe the basket contents.

ASSEMBLING THE GIFT BASKET

1. Create a base in the basket with brown paper.
2. Arrange the items in the basket.
3. Wrap with cellophane. Top with a black and white polka-dot bow. Glue a yellow button at the center. ❏

HARVEST PEARS
gift basket

Fruit baskets may well have been the first gift baskets as neighbors shared an abundant harvest. This simple basket is decorated with stems and leaves from a silk flower stem so any fruit can be displayed. Present lemons and oranges, peaches and apples, or whatever your garden offers. The decorated basket is wonderful for displaying fruit in the kitchen.

SUPPLIES

Basket:
Natural round wicker basket, 9" diameter, 3 1/2" high

Basket Decorations:
• Silk stems and leaves
• Raffia and large-eye needle
• Cellophane wrap

Gift Basket Contents:
• Fresh pears (or any other fruit)
• Natural excelsior

DECORATING THE BASKET

You can leave the leaves on the stem or cut them off now and attach them with a glue gun later.

1. With wire cutters, remove some of the wicker so you can push the stem in the basket to create the handles. For additional security, use a piece of raffia threaded in a large-eye needle to stitch the stems in place.
2. Wrap other stem pieces around the base and the rim of the basket.
3. Glue any leaves to balance the arrangement or, if you cut the leaves off the stems, glue them in place.

ASSEMBLING THE GIFT BASKET

1. Fill the bottom of the basket with natural wood excelsior. (No base is needed.)
2. Fill with fruit.
3. *Option:* Wrap the basket with cellophane. ❑

GARDENING GROWS THE SPIRIT
gift basket

This basket full of gardening items is a perfect "Welcome to Your New Home" or "Welcome Spring" gift. If you include a live plant, leave some vents in the cellophane wrapping to prevent condensation inside the cellophane.

SUPPLIES

Basket:

Low splint rectangle basket with handles, 12" x 16" x 10"

Basket Decorations:

- Medium brown wood stain *or* brown acrylic paint + gel medium in a 50/50 mix
- Dark brown stain *or* dark brown acrylic paint + gel medium in a 50/50 mix
- Brush
- 2 yards jute garden twine
- Acrylic craft paints - Light green, medium green, antique white Paint brush and sponge
- Silver label holder
- Black permanent marker
- Green raffia
- Cellophane wrap

continued on page 106

continued from page 104

Gift Basket Contents:

- Floral foam brick
- Brown kraft paper
- Natural excelsior
- Seed packages, a burlap sack of bulbs, a plant
- Garden tools - Garden twine, plant markers, garden shears, gardening gloves
- Clay pots
- *Nice Additions:* A book about gardening, instructions for planting the bulbs

DECORATING THE BASKET

1. Stain the basket inside and out with the medium brown stain. Let dry.

2. To give the basket a weathered look, sponge the green paints in patches on the handle and basket bottom.

3. With a pencil, mark where the label holder will go. Paint that space with antique white paint.

4. Stain the entire basket, including the white and green patches, with dark brown stain. (This gives an antique look and blends and tones the colors.)

5. Wrap the tops of the handles with jute twine.

6. Attach the label holder over the white patch with metal glue. *Option:* If the rim is wide enough, add two small nails to help secure the label holder.

7. Inside the label holder, write *le jardin* (French for "the garden") with a black marker.

ASSEMBLING THE GIFT BASKET

1. Cut a brick of floral foam in half. Place the plant in the middle of the basket and secure firmly with floral foam and brown paper to create the base. Cover with natural wood excelsior.

2. Place the other objects into the basket.

3. Wrap the basket with cellophane, leaving the sides open for ventilation.

4. Top with a green raffia bow. ❏

LA LAVENDER
garden basket

This basket holds a lavender plant, a drying rack, and items made with lavender. It's perfect for a gardener or cooking enthusiast who would appreciate its potential, and shows how almost any theme can be the inspiration for a gift basket!

The vintage-look basket can be used as a market basket or flower gathering basket after the items are removed.

continued from page 108

SUPPLIES

Basket:

Large wicker oval market basket with handle, 16" x 8" x 10" high

Basket Decorations:

- Acrylic craft paints - Green, light blue
- Dark brown stain *or* dark brown acrylic paint + acrylic gel medium in a 50/50 mix
- Large basecoating brush
- 100 grit sandpaper
- Purple polymer clay
- Alphabet rubber stamps
- 2 small metal eyelets
- Wire
- Cellophane wrap

Gift Basket Contents:

- Brown kraft paper
- Natural excelsior
- Lavender plant
- Dried lavender bundle
- Garden shears
- Lavender Drying Rack (instructions follow)
- Lavender Cookies and recipe (recipe follows)
- Instructions for harvesting and drying lavender (included below)

DECORATING THE BASKET

Paint & Stain:

1. Paint the outside of the basket with green acrylic paint. While still wet, color wash a few patches of light blue paint, blending them into the green.
2. Paint the handle with light blue paint. Let dry.
3. Stain the outside of the basket and the handle with

How to Harvest and Dry Lavender

This rubber band method is quick and holds the bunch securely while drying. If you use string or raffia, when the stems shrink your flowers and leaves will end up all over the floor. A rubber band holds the bunch tightly during the whole drying process.

1. For maximum oil content, cut the lavender stalks when the dew has dried and the flowers have just opened.
2. Strip off the leaves at the bottom of the stem where the bunch will be bound. (This increases the strength of the stems and speeds drying.)
3. Gather a small bunch of stems (12 to 16). Making sure they have sufficient air circulation, secure with a rubber band.
4. Take the bound bunch and slip part of the rubber band over a hook on the drying rack. Let dry.

To use: Rub the stems in your hands to release the fragrance. ❏

dark brown stain. Let dry completely.

4. Distress the basket with sandpaper, sanding away the paint and stain places to reveal the original wicker color.

Make & Attach the Label:

1. Make a label from purple polymer clay, following the instructions in the Techniques section. Impress the label with the word LAVENDER, using alphabet rubber stamps and push small metal eyelets into the ends of the label. Bake and cool according to the clay manufacturer's instructions.
2. Lightly dry brush the label with light blue paint to highlight the lettering.
3. Attach the label to the basket with wire, twisting the ends inside the basket to hold firmly.

ASSEMBLING THE GIFT BASKET

1. Place the lavender plant in one side of the basket.
2. Fill the other side with brown paper and natural wooden excelsior to create a base.
3. Place the drying rack (secured to the handle with glue dots, if necessary), lavender bundle, cookies, and shears in the basket.
4. *Optional:* Wrap with cellophane. Be sure to leave vents to prevent condensation from the live plant. ❏

PROJECT

Lavender Drying Rack

Use the same colors you used for the basket for a coordinated look. The handmade wire hooks are easy and charming.

Supplies:
Oval wooden plaque, 14" x 2-1/2"
Acrylic craft paints - Green, light blue, dusty purple
Black crafting wire
7 upholstery tacks

Here's How:
1. Paint the plaque with green paint. Let dry.
2. Color wash with light blue.
3. Paint the trim with dusty purple. Let dry.
4. Use crafting wire to form four hooks in a simple fleur de lis shape.
5. Attach each wire hook to the plaque with a tack, spacing them evenly. Place a tack between each hook. ❑

RECIPE

Lavender Sugar Cookies

*This recipe yields two dozen cookies. CAUTION: Use **only** lavender you grew yourself or lavender from the herb section of a health food store. **Do NOT use** potpourri.*

Ingredients:
1 cup butter, room temperature
2/3 cup sugar
2 large eggs, beaten
1 teaspoon vanilla extract
2 cups all-purpose flour
3 to 4 tablespoons fresh lavender florets or 2 tablespoons dried lavender
Superfine sugar

Here's How:
1. Cream together butter and sugar until light and fluffy.
2. Mix eggs into the butter-and-sugar mixture.
3. Stir in flour and lavender until mixture becomes a soft ball. Cover ball of dough and place in refrigerator 15 minutes. Preheat oven 375 degrees F.
4. Remove dough from refrigerator. On a lightly sugared surface, roll dough approximately 1/4" thick. Cut into shapes with cookie cutters and place on ungreased cookie sheets.
5. Bake 12 to 15 minutes or until cookies are lightly browned around the edges. Remove from oven and let cool on wire racks. ❑

THANK YOU BERRY MUCH
gift basket

This large-slat basket was a perfect surface for fabric decoupage. I chose a large print fabric with hydrangeas and berries - it gives a homey elegance and looks handpainted. The basket holds homemade berry jam.

continued from page 112

SUPPLIES

Basket:

Round wooden splint basket, original handle removed, 9" diameter, 7" high

Basket Decorations:

- Gold metallic spray paint
- 100% cotton fabric for decoupage and to make enough fabric ribbon for two bows
- Decoupage medium
- Stems of artificial berries and leaves
- Acrylic craft paint - Dark green
- Gold tassel
- 1 yard garden twine
- Wire
- Cellophane wrap

Gift Basket Contents:

- Floral foam brick
- Brown kraft paper
- Natural excelsior
- Homemade jams

DECORATING THE BASKET

Paint:

1. Paint the inside of the basket with two coats of gold spray paint.
2. Paint the rim of the basket with dark green acrylic paint. Let dry.

Decoupage:

1. Cut the fabric into 24 strips, each 3" x 9". TIP: If you're using a fabric with large motifs, keep the strips in order so the print will match as you apply them to the basket. (If you choose a small-motif print, you won't need to worry about keeping the strips in order.)
2. Coat the back of one fabric strip with decoupage medium and position on the basket. (See the decoupage

---

PROJECT

Decorating Jam Jars

Use scraps of the stiffened fabric you made for the fabric ribbon to decorate the jam jars.

Supplies:
Jars of jam
Stiffened fabric
Scissors
Glue
Labels
Berry charms

Here's How:
1. Using a lid liner as a template, cut circles from the stiffened fabric.
2. Glue to the jar lids.
3. Cut 1/2" strips of fabric. Glue around the rims of the lids.
4. Add a pretty label and a berry charm to each jar. ❑

---

instruction in the Techniques section for more details.) Smooth out any wrinkles and apply another coat of decoupage medium. Continue around the basket, keeping the strips in order and slightly over-lapping them. Let dry completely before proceeding.

Add Handle:

1. Make a handle from the artificial stems with the berries and leaves still attached. Push the ends of the stems in the basket and secure with wire. Glue additional stems along the basket rim and secure with wire. Glue leaves to hide any wire that shows. If needed, glue on additional leaves and berries to complete the arrangement.
2. Wrap the stems together at the top of the handle with garden twine.

Make & Attach Bow:

1. Make a multi-loop bow with 1/2" fabric ribbon made from the same fabric you covered the basket with. See the Techniques section for instructions on making fabric ribbon.
2. Attach the bow at the base of the handle. Loop on the tassel. Glue a few berries and leaves to the center of the bow.

ASSEMBLING THE GIFT BASKET

1. Cut a brick of floral foam to fit in the basket and create a sturdy, level base for the jars. Add brown paper around the floral foam, if needed.

2. Add natural wood excelsior. Position the jars of jam.

3. Wrap the basket in cellophane and finish the top with a matching fabric ribbon bow. ❏

GOLDEN GRAPES
wine basket

This seagrass basket is the perfect size to hold and present a single bottle. Artificial fruits are widely available at craft outlets and can be easily arranged around the basket rim.

I used a grapes-and-wine theme for this basket; you could substitute a fruit syrup for the wine and use another fruit theme. Flavored fruit syrups are scrumptious and easy to make. They can be used for topping pancakes, waffles, French toast, ice cream, or desserts (another great way to share a harvest!). The syrups are packaged in bottles like wine bottles and can be substituted for wine in any bottle basket.

SUPPLIES

Basket:

Round coiled seagrass basket with
  side handles, 6" diameter, 5" high

Basket Decorations:

• Artificial grapes

• Gold metallic acrylic paint

• Painting sponge

• Spray-on floral foam

• Brass embossed tag

• Metallic gold wire-edge ribbon,
  1/4" wide

• Metallic gold net ribbon, 3" wide

• Gold cord with tassels at ends

• Cellophane wrap

Gift Basket Contents:

• Recycled paper shreds

• Gold metallic shreds

• Bottle of white wine *or* Flavored
  Fruit Syrup (recipe follows)

RECIPE
Flavored Fruit Syrup

It takes only minutes to prepare a fruit syrup in a microwave oven or on the stove. Fruit possibilities include raspberries, blackberries, blueberries, strawberries, and purple plums. Package the syrup in clean wine bottles. Once opened, syrup can be kept in the refrigerator for six months.

Ingredients:
4 cups fresh fruit *or* two 16-ounce bags of frozen fruit
2 cups sugar
1-1/2 cups light corn syrup

Procedure
1. Place clean, empty bottles in a pan and cover with boiling water.
2. Place the fruit in a large microwave-safe bowl. Cover with plastic wrap and microwave on high for 10 to 12 minutes or until boiling, stirring every 3 minutes. *Option:* Heat the fruit on the stovetop over medium heat until boiling; stir constantly to prevent scorching.
3. Line a strainer with cheesecloth and place the strainer in a large bowl. Pour in hot fruit and mash the fruit with a spoon to press the juice through the strainer. You should have 1 to 1-1/2 cups of juice. Discard the pulp.
4. Add the sugar and corn syrup to the fruit juice. Microwave on high for 5 to 8 minutes or until boiling, stirring every 2 minutes. *Option:* Cook on the stove until boiling, stirring constantly.
5. Boil hard for 1 minute. Skim off any foam from the top.
6. Pour the syrup into hot, sterilized bottles. Seal with a new cork or a screw-top lid. ❑

Golden Grapes, continued

DECORATING THE BASKET

1. Gild the grapes by spraying them lightly with gold paint. Let dry.

2. Apply spray-on floral foam to the rim of the basket. Insert sprigs of grapes and leaves in foam. Let set.

ASSEMBLING THE GIFT BASKET

1. Place recycled paper shreds in the basket to lift up the bottle and secure it in place. Place gold metallic shreds on top.

2. Tie the brass tag to the handles.

3. Wrap the basket in cellophane. Embellish with a large bow made from 3" wide gold net ribbon and a cord with tassels. ❏

CHAMPAGNE DREAMS
gift basket

SUPPLIES

Basket:

Round wicker basket without handle, 7" diameter, 7" high

Basket Decorations:

• Whitewash *or* white acrylic paint + gel medium in a 50/50 mix
• 100 grit sandpaper
• Aluminum tag
• 1 yard thin metallic silver ribbon
• White tulle
• Silk magnolia flower

Gift Basket Contents:

• Bottle of champagne
• Recycled paper shreds
• Natural excelsior

DECORATING THE BASKET

1. Whitewash basket. Let dry.

2. Rub basket with sandpaper for a distressed look. Wipe away dust.

3. Emboss the metal tag with the couple's initial(s) and set aside. See the Techniques section for embossing instructions.

ASSEMBLING THE GIFT BASKET

1. Add recycled shreds to the basket to make a nest for the bottle. Top with natural excelsior.

2. Position bottle in basket.

3. Wrap with tulle.

4. Arrange the silk magnolia and leaves at the top of the bottle.

5. Attach the tag with silver ribbon. ❏

This beautiful presentation of a single bottle is elegant and memorable. Give a bottle of champagne to a newlywed couple with instructions that it be opened on their first anniversary. You could also present a bottle of good brandy with instructions to open it on their twenty-fifth anniversary! Be sure to include storage information, if appropriate.

119

FRIENDSHIP IS THE WINE OF LIFE
wine basket

Here's a basket for wine lovers with the makings for a romantic evening - wine, glasses, candles and holders, even the napkins. It's a nice gift for people who've just moved, for an anniversary, or to say thank you.

SUPPLIES

Basket:

Round wicker basket, 11" diameter, 3-1/2" high

Basket Decorations:

• Whitewash *or* white acrylic paint + gel medium in a 50/50 mix
• 100 grit sandpaper
• 1 yard white crocheted lace trim, 3" wide
• 1 yard green-and-white checked ribbon, 1/4" wide
• 1 yard green-and-white checked ribbon, 1-1/2" wide
• White ribbon roses
• Cellophane wrap

Gift Basket Contents:

• Brown kraft paper
• Cream pleated paper shreds
• Wood skewer
• Silk ivy leaves
• Polymer clay and seal to decorate wine bottle
• Bottle of wine
• Wineglasses
• Candles and candleholders
• Paper cocktail napkins

DECORATING THE BASKET

1. Whitewash the basket, applying two coats. Let dry.

2. Bring out the weave of the basket by distressing with sandpaper. Wipe away dust.

3. Using a needle and thread, tack the white ribbon to the rim of the basket every 1-1/2", leaving a little slack so the ribbon poofs out.

4. Glue a ribbon rose over each stitched space.

5. Thread the thin ribbon through the crocheted lace. Using a glue gun, glue the lace around the inside of the basket.

ASSEMBLING THE GIFT BASKET

1. Decorate the bottle of wine with a polymer clay seal tied on with a piece of ribbon. See the Techniques section for instructions on working with polymer clay.

2. Place the wine bottle in the middle of the basket and secure in a brown paper base. *TIP:* Use a few glue dots on the bottom of the bottle to prevent it from tipping.

3. Top the base with cream pleated paper shreds.

4. Tie the stems of the glasses together with ribbon and place in the basket.

5. Tie the candles with ribbon and place in the basket.

6. Tie the napkins with ribbon. Glue on a wooden skewer and prop them upright behind the bottle of wine.

7. Add a few sprigs of variegated silk ivy as accents. Wrap with cellophane. Top with a matching bow and a sprig of ivy. ❏

MUCHOS MARGARITAS
gift basket

A tray basket provides a flat base to build the gift and is useful and attractive. Because the bottle and glasses could tip over easily in this type of basket, use glue dots for attaching them to the tray without harming the surface.

continued from page 125

SUPPLIES

Basket:

Wicker basket tray, 11" x 15" x 2-1/2" high

Basket Decorations:

• Plastic or glass sheet, clear or pale blue, 10" x 14"

• Decoupage paper with shell motifs

• Decoupage medium

• Scissors

• Glue dots

• Brush

• Cellophane wrap

• Natural raffia

• Silk orchid

Gift Basket Contents:

• Clear tape

• Natural excelsior

• Bottle of tequila

• Liquor bottle pouring spouts

• Margarita mix, tin of margarita salt, fresh limes

• Margarita glasses

• Glass charms (instructions follow)

PROJECT
Glass Charms

Use a different shell for each glass charm so guests can easily identify their drinks at the party!

Supplies:
Beads - six to eight per charm, in a variety of shapes, sizes, and green hues
Shells - one per charm, drilled with a small hole
Silver wire loop earring finding - one per charm
Silver crimp beads - two per charm
Silver jump ring - 1 per charm

Here's How:
1. Remove the thin wire piece from the earring finding by clipping it off with wire cutters.
2. Thread the shell on a silver jump ring. Place on the loop. Thread three to four beads on each side of the shell. To prevent the beads from coming off, attach a crimp bead at each end of the wire loop. Squeeze hard with pliers to keep them firmly in place.

To use: Loop around the stem of the glass. ❏

DECORATING THE BASKET

1. Cut out shell motifs from the decoupage paper. Using decoupage medium, apply them to the underside of the plastic sheet. Let dry completely.

2. Place plastic sheet in the bottom of the tray.

To clean: Wipe the surface with a damp cloth. **Never** immerse the decoupaged tray bottom in water.

ASSEMBLING THE GIFT BASKET

1. Secure the bottle, drink mix, and glasses to the bottom of the tray with glue dots. TIP: Use clear tape to tape the glasses together to prevent them from knocking against each other and possibly chipping.

2. Place natural wood excelsior in the bottom of the tray. Arrange other gift items.

3. Wrap with cellophane. Top with a natural raffia bow. Place a tropical orchid at the center of the bow. ❏

METRIC CONVERSION CHART

Inches to Millimeters and Centimeters

Inches	MM	CM	Inches	MM	CM
1/8	3	.3	2	51	5.1
1/4	6	.6	3	76	7.6
3/8	10	1.0	4	102	10.2
1/2	13	1.3	5	127	12.7
5/8	16	1.6	6	152	15.2
3/4	19	1.9	7	178	17.8
7/8	22	2.2	8	203	20.3
1	25	2.5	9	229	22.9
1-1/4	32	3.2	10	254	25.4
1-1/2	38	3.8	11	279	27.9
1-3/4	44	4.4	12	305	30.5

Yards to Meters

Yards	Meters	Yards	Meters
1/8	.11	3	2.74
1/4	.23	4	3.66
3/8	.34	5	4.57
1/2	.46	6	5.49
5/8	.57	7	6.40
3/4	.69	8	7.32
7/8	.80	9	8.23
1	.91	10	9.14
2	1.83		

INDEX

Continued on next page